MEN IN THE BIBLE

Also by John F. O'Grady
Published by Paulist Press

According to John

Catholic Beliefs and Traditions

The Four Gospels and the Jesus Tradition

Models of Jesus Revisited

Pillars of Paul's Gospel: Galatians and Romans

The Roman Catholic Church: Its Origin and Nature

MEN IN THE BIBLE

THE GOOD THE BAD & THE UGLY

JOHN F. O'GRADY

Paulist Press
New York/Mahwah, N.J.

Cover design by Kevin van der Leek Design

Book design by Sharyn Banks

Library of Congress Cataloging-in-Publication Data

O'Grady, John F.
    Men in the Bible : the good, the bad, and the ugly / John F. O'Grady.
        p. cm.
    Includes bibliographical references.
    ISBN 0-8091-4262-7 (alk. paper)
1. Men in the Bible—Biography. 2. Bible—Biography. I. Title.

    BS574.5.O37 2005
    220.9′2′081—dc22   2004022081

Published by Paulist Press
997 Macarthur Boulevard
Mahwah, New Jersey 07430

www.paulistpress.com

Printed and bound in the
United States of America

Contents

Contents

...your old men shall dream dreams,
and your young men shall see visions.
—Joel 2:28

For Some Dreamers and Visionaries:

The Rev. Dr. George J. Dyer, visionary and dreamer, on the occasion of his fiftieth anniversary as a priest

Dr. Charles R. Modica who had a vision of St. George's University

Dr. Michael J. Griffin who dreamed and completed his doctorate

Joseph P. O'Grady, Jr., who has both visions and dreams

Preface

People make history. Events may shape people but individual personalities color the events. People and their stories fascinate with their greatness and their pettiness. People go through life with ups and downs and sideway movements. Trying to predict or chart a course leads often to failure. Life must be lived and not feared or run from. Experiencing the depths of human failures can often lead to the heights of human ecstasy. Drinking deeply of the wine of life makes the water of life seem insipid even if the water is sobering. Such is the situation of the individuals in the Bible. Each has a story to tell.

In this book I have chosen six men from the Old Testament and six men from the New Testament. Those chosen form part of my personal life. I like them and always have since I first read the Bible. I have other friends from the Bible, both men and women, and I hope to write about them as well in the future.

While all twelve individuals, even Judas, are my friends, I like some more than others. This the reader will easily detect. Although Adam was a wimp, I still like him. And although David was a great sinner, I have always followed the example of God and loved David. For me, Moses remains the creation of Cecil B. DeMille, and DeMille's depiction of Moses, although containing much fantasy, still appeals to the imagination of a person of faith. Isaiah has long been part of my heart as the eternal optimist and I like the way Jeremiah deals with God and God deals with him.

Jesus, of course, has long been the object of my literary pursuit as well as my personal pursuer. I especially like the inability of any evangelist to adequately depict his many-faceted life and person. Peter attracts because of his bravado coupled with failure. I have loved both Paul and the Beloved Disciple and would like to think that I have learned much from their personal qualities. John the Baptist appeals because he tells the truth and is honest with himself. These qualities I often find personally elusive. And finally, there is the tragic Judas. Jesus offered him so much and Judas failed so miserably. Some may think I want to rehabilitate this flawed and fallen apostle. No, I do not wish to rehabilitate. I just want to tell the story with as much sympathy as possible. I do believe that "Father, forgive them for they know not what they do" applies to Judas—and also to me and countless others.

This book grew out of a course at Barry University. Both men and women undergraduates actually read Genesis, Exodus, 1 and 2 Samuel, 1 Chronicles, Isaiah, and Jeremiah from the Old Testament, and the four gospels as well as some of Paul's writings. These students did so because they wanted to learn about the people. Some they liked and some they did not like. Both men and women in the class liked Jeremiah. Many of the men in the class liked David, but not too many women had kind thoughts about David. All the students became fascinated with the different ways the four evangelists depicted Jesus and usually Luke and John won the popularity context. Readers will have their own favorites from both the Old Testament and the New Testament.

Some of this book was written in Rome. Most was written in Miami. I live in three places regularly: Miami, Rome, and Voorheesville, New York. I am not sure how much of my life in each place is real and how much is unreal. I know only that each is part of me and each has supported me in my pursuit of the Bible. People in each place make my life better just as each person in the Bible has made me happier and a better person. How much of the Bible is real and how much unreal? It is all real for it records the wanderings in faith of men and women, just as all of the people in the three places in my life join a communal wandering in faith. The unreality points only to the true reality.

Preface

Gratitude to others always constitutes anything I have accomplished. Once again I acknowledge my indebtedness to Dr. Mary Ann Jungbauer who continues to improve what I write by her careful proofreading. The former Dean of the School of Arts and Sciences, Dr. Laura Armesto, and the Chair of the Theology Department the Rev. Dr. Mark Wedig, OP, have graciously adjusted my schedule to allow me time to spend in Rome each year. I remain grateful to them. Finally, I have personally learned much from reading about and studying these men in the Bible. I hope the same will be true for those who read this book.

Miami, Florida
June 29, Feast of Sts. Peter and Paul

Images of God
in the Bible

A book on men in the Bible must include some understanding of God in the Bible. Otherwise, the reader has little to use in understanding how these individual men responded to the many serious questions of life. Hebrew words can offer sufficient understanding of the Hebrew God to lay the foundation for the human understanding of God and how individual men responded to these images of God. Of course, women related to these same images but as in most aspects of life, women often respond differently from men to the same stimuli and images. And as also true in life, many times the Bible presents women in a subordinate and often inferior role.

The God of History

The first couple related to God on an intimate and comfortable level. The presence of evil in the world changed that level of comfort but did not destroy it. Actually throughout the Bible as God continues to offer a relationship to men and to women, people had different images of just what God is like. History and the relationship of God to human history constitute one overriding dimension of the biblical deity. People get to know God through their own history. The movement advances from Abraham to Moses to Judges, to Kings and to Prophets, and finally to Jesus. God functions differently during this history: creator and general, father and mother, judge and shepherd, and even as husband. In

1

all, God promises a good future in the presence of human failure and tragedy (Brueggemann: 145–213).

In Exodus Moses asks the name of God:

> "If I come to the people of Israel and say to them, 'The God of your fathers has sent me to you,' and they ask me, 'What is his name?' what shall I say to them?" God said to Moses, *"ehyeh asher ehyeh."* (Exod 3:13–14a)

Hebrew has no fully developed system of tenses similar to English. The principal tenses are actions completed and actions not completed. The Hebrew words quoted above refer to action not completed and thus can be translated two ways; "I am who I am" or "I will be who I will be." The second seems preferable since Hebrew has no great interest in philosophy or metaphysics (Fretheim, 1992: 62–65). People will learn the God of the Bible in their history. The God of the Bible offers a relationship in the historical events of everyday human life. "God will be what God will be." God will be present in the chaos of history offering a special relationship to the people of Israel, with promises for the future and qualities of God which will become characteristics of the people of God.

tohu we bohu

Ancient peoples vehemently disliked disorder. They faced it too often and knew its destructive force. They feared disorder in creation and they suffered because of it. Without a sense of control and the ordinary ebb and flow of daily life, human existence passed more quickly than necessary. They knew, however, that chaos and disorder lurked in every corner, in every time, and every place, ready to strike against the endless efforts to keep it under control.

The author of Genesis proclaimed that in the beginning God created the world out of chaos, disorder:

> The earth was without form and void *(tohu we bohu),*
> and darkness was upon the face of the deep and the Spirit

> of God was moving over the face of the waters. And God
> said, "Let there be light"; and there was light. (Gen 1:2–3)

The spirit of God moved over the chaos and brought order from
disorder. Then God gave it to *ahdam* to continue the struggle
against *tohu we bohu*. Both male and female would continue the
battle as they exercised dominion over all of creation. They
accepted responsibility to fight against *tohu we bohu*. Civilizations
would rise when ordinary people continued to control chaos and
reacted against disorder. Civilizations would fall when people gave
up the effort. Chaos would have won.

Desert a room or a building and slowly, and then quickly, *tohu
we bohu* will take over. The room decays, the building falls apart,
and all will return to formless waste. Dust and dirt creep in and
eventually cover all. Observe abandoned buildings along rivers,
long ago used for commerce. Only frames and building blocks
remain. The inner city's structures decay because no one cares for
them and no one takes the time and money to maintain them. Eventually even without the human scavengers, they will all fall into
decay. *Tohu we bohu* thrives in the twenty-first century as it did in
the ancient world. *Tohu we bohu* lurks everywhere. *Tohu we bohu*
lives in the disorder of personal life, in the confusion of relationships, in the marketplace of daily existence. People will struggle
against *tohu we bohu* as well, until the day they must give up and
the body too becomes part of the eternal return to formless waste.
The God of the Bible has given the Spirit, which helps individuals
and groups to overcome chaos that surrounds all. God likes order.
God has implanted order in the universe and when people find and
live according to this order, *tohu we bohu* vanishes.

Berith

Anyone who has read the Bible knows the word *covenant*
(Mendenhall: 1179–1202). Few beyond the Jewish community
know the Hebrew word for covenant, *berith*. In English a

"covenant" usually means an agreement between two parties in which both promise to do or not do certain actions. Consequences usually follow if one of the parties fails to uphold the promise. The English word *covenant* functions as a major metaphor in explaining the relationship offered by God to people. Therein lies the trouble. People today cannot easily understand a relationship based on a promise. Relationships are based on blood, or legal peculiarities, or business situations, or on physical qualities, or even on emotional need. A promise as a basis for a relationship seems too little or too much. Such a fragile or demanding foundation for a relationship becomes evident when the promise lies broken in history. How can the relationship survive?

In the history of Israel the single word *berith* came to cover a number of types of relationships and promises. Treaties, loyalty oaths, charters, promises—all fell under the one word, along with conditional promises and unconditional promises. The promises often took on a socially enacted historical reality expected to affect behavioral changes, as well as formal symbolic and even dogmatic promises that became the object of tradition and belief. Some conditional elements became associated with the former and unconditional elements associated with the latter. The first type were bilateral and the second type unilateral.

Covenants

> Covenant of Noah: Genesis 9:8–17
> Covenant of Abraham: Genesis 15:18
> Covenant of Moses: Sinai: Exodus 19:1–8;
>   Horeb: Exodus 33:6–23
> Covenant of Joshua: Joshua 24:16–25
> Covenant of David: 2 Samuel 7, 23:5

Each covenant has some constant elements and other aspects which differ one from the other. Some involve historical figures and others seem to come from legends. The constant and singularly important element is the promise of God. All else may fail but God remains faithful. *Berith* also contained a sense of responsibility but not primarily on the part of the human partner. If such responsibility fell on the human race, the promise and the relationship was doomed to failure. The relationship to God could continue only if God assumed the primary responsibility, which the God of the Bible willingly seems to have done. In the midst of continual and continuous human failure, God never abandoned the relationship with the chosen people (Boadt: 174–76). God had promised, and even if the human part of the relationship failed to live up to what God hoped for, God remained the faithful one.

Some prefer to understand *berith* as a charter (Mendenhall: 1188). God conferred a privilege, dignity, and power and status on people. Three unconditional charters appear in the Bible: Noah, Abraham, and David. Although the promise to David is not called a *berith* in Samuel, its interpretation throughout the Bible has always considered it a *berith*. Both Noah and Abraham specified it as *berith*. Here, however, the promise is unilateral on the part of God. God and not human beings are bound by oath. God promises to Noah and all on the ark the assurance that they need never again fear such a devastating flood. God promised to Abraham and his offspring the land and great progeny. God promised to David and his dynasty perpetual rule. All are unconditional and act as theology rather than as historical events in which both parties assume mutual responsibilities.

Most people see the Sinai covenant and Joshua different from the above three. Here the relationship seems more conditional, even using conditional terms: "…teach them the statutes and instructions and make known to them the way they are to go and the things they are to do" (Exod 18:20). *Torah* (instruction) gives to the people of Israel numerous commandments and the observance of these commands will constitute them as the holy people of God.

The God of the Old Testament never reneged on this responsibility established by God and on God. However, this same God expected the people to be priestly, to be the one chosen people elected to be a sign of God's salvation to all nations. This people offered to God the worship of the heart and never was supposed to separate their election from the call to take care of those in need. God expected the people of Israel to respond to the offer of a relationship based on the promise made, but even when *they* failed, the God of the Old Testament never changed.

The holy nation and the kingdom of priests applied to all Israelites, to all Jews. Their destiny involved not only a special relationship to God but also a responsibility to all other peoples. Priests act in the name of people in the presence of God. They act in God's name, making people aware of the saving presence of God in all of human life. Such was the call of Israel by the God of the Old Testament.

Sign of Salvation to the Nations

Other nations and cultures were meant to recognize in Israel the presence of the one true God. They were to stream into the city of Jerusalem to learn of this God, and with worship share in the saving presence of God in human history. The priest makes the divine manifest in human history. The priest joins heaven to earth and earth to heaven. The priest mediates between divinity and humanity. The books of Exodus and Deuteronomy offer the foundation for the priesthood of all believers in Israel.

> Now therefore, if you will obey my voice and keep my covenant, you shall be my own possession among all peoples; for all the earth is mine, and you shall be to me a kingdom of priests and a holy nation. (Exod 19:5–6)

> ...but you who cling to the LORD your God, are all alive today. Therefore I teach you the statutes and decrees as the LORD my God has commanded me, that you may observe them in the land you are entering to occupy. Observe them carefully, so thus will you give

evidence of your wisdom and intelligence to the nations, who will hear all of these statutes and say: "This great nation is truly a wise and intelligent people." (Deut 4:4–6)

For you are a people sacred to the LORD, your God who has chosen you from all the nations on the face of the earth to be a people peculiarly his own. (Deut 14:2)

He will then raise you high in praise and renown and glory above all other nations he has made, and you will be a people sacred to the LORD your God, as he promised. (Deut 26:19)

True Worship

The God of the Old Testament expected the chosen people, unlike other nations—that engaged in often bizarre sacrifices, including human sacrifice—to offer the only true worship, the worship of the heart. God did not want holocausts but the offering of a "humble and contrite heart."

> For you are not pleased with sacrifices;
> should I offer a holocaust, you would not accept it.
> My sacrifice, O God, is a contrite spirit;
> a heart contrite and humbled, O God, you will not
> spurn. (Ps 51:16–17)

Sacrifices of bulls and grain offerings please only if they express in ritual form the offering of a life lived for God and for God's people. Without this heart of the sacrifice, all such offerings become ritual lies, an abomination to the Lord.

Care for the Poor

The God of the Old Testament also expected people to accept an obligation to care for the poor, the forgotten, the abandoned, those who had no one else on whom they could rely and trust. The unfortunate of the earth would become the special care of God's people. The poor and all who help the poor would live together with complete dependence on the power and goodness of God. As the people of Israel were once abandoned and in need of freedom and liberation and justice in Egypt, so these same people must always remember the history and condition of old, and care for the needs of others.

> The needy will never be lacking in the land; that is why I command you to open your hand to your poor and needy kinsmen in your country. (Deut 15:11)

God would bless the people if they took care of those in need (Deut 15:1–11). A nation that had benefited from the goodness and benevolence of God should always carefully look after the less fortunate. Such practices please God and ensure continued blessings. When Israel fulfilled this role, it would flourish as a holy nation, and other peoples would come to the holy city of Jerusalem and offer to Israel the dignity and honor due to the nation that revealed the mystery of God's plan for all creation.

> Nations shall walk by your light
>   and kings by your radiance.
> Raise your eyes and look about;
>   they all gather and come to you,
> your sons come from afar
>   and your daughters in the arms of their nurses.
>   (Isa 60:3–4)

To support the chosen people, God expressed certain qualities toward Israel. Covenantal virtues characterized all of the dealings of God with the chosen nation. The *hesed* and *emeth* of God bound together both participants in the covenant. As a result, the Old Testament overflows with references to these two covenantal virtues.

The LORD has made his salvation known,
  in the sight of the nations he has revealed his justice.
He has remembered his kindness and his faithfulness
  toward the house of Israel.
All the ends of the earth have seen the salvation by our
  God. (Ps 98:2–3)

Hesed

The Hebrew word *hesed* cannot be adequately translated into English (Zobel: 44–64). Sometimes translators will use the word *compassion,* at other times *kindness,* and sometimes *mercy.* Each English word conveys some insight into the wealth of meaning in this small Hebrew word. The God of the Bible is a compassionate God. The compassionate person enters into the experience of the other and if the experience is good, the moment is doubly enjoyed. If the experience is bad or painful, the sorrow is more easily borne through the presence of the compassionate person. God was compassionate with Israel, entering into the joys and sadness, celebrating the good times, and helping to bear the sorrow. The God of the Bible treated the chosen people with kindness. The kind person emphasizes the positive, seeking the good and always overlooking the evil. God always saw the good in the people of Israel and even if he punished them, eventually the kind God turned to forgiveness. Everyone has failed, has sinned, and has missed the mark. The God of the Bible knew the sins and failures of people and always forgave. God held no grudges. Punishing the people of Israel for a time, God always relented and restored the people, promising eventually an eternal restoration and fulfillment.

Emeth

Emeth likewise causes problems for the translators. Sometimes the word in English becomes *truth,* or *fidelity,* or means something that is perduring or enduring (McKenzie: 267, 901). Fidelity seems the best translation. God remains faithful to the chosen people no matter what. The fidelity of God outlasts all human fidelity and puts to shame any human attempt to remain faithful in the midst of betrayal and rejection. God always remains faithful in the midst of human infidelity, for God remains God. Humans might react differently in the midst of infidelity but God must continue as the faithful one, otherwise human failure controls God. Divinity demands fidelity. Once God has spoken, the word remains. The history of Israel is the history of failure on the part of the chosen people, and the history of the eternal, perduring, enduring compassion, kindness, and forgiveness of God.

Kabod

The Bible also speaks of the glory of God (McKenzie: 313–14). *Kabod* (glory) etymologically signifies weight or heaviness and can be applied to both people and God. When applied to God in the Old Testament the issue becomes rather complex, with a mixture of sophisticated theology and concrete manifestations. The most primitive form of glory in the Pentateuch involved light and the pillar of cloud. Both fire and the cloud were concrete manifestations in the Exodus tradition of the presence and protection of God. When the Israelites saw the cloud (Exod 16:10; 24:16–18; Lev 9:6, 23) or the pillar of fire, they knew that God was near and they felt secure. Later in the prophets the glory of God covered Israel like a canopy, a protection against all evil and evildoers (Isa 4:5; 58:8; Mic 1:15).

Frequently the glory includes light. Thus, "the earth is full of the glory of God" refers to the light that creation contains and manifests. The presence of light in contrast to the darkness, also present in creation, reminds the Israelites of the presence and protection of their God. In later books glory loses some of its concrete meaning and to see the glory of God means to see and experience the saving deeds of God (Isa 35:2; 40:5; 59:19; 66:18–19; Ps 63:3). The glory of God manifests who God is and this becomes evident in what God has done for the people. God is glorified when the goodness and power of God become manifest. Historically the Exodus experience manifests in a paramount way the glory of God. God's power overcomes the power of pharaoh; God's goodness takes a captive people and gives them freedom and a land. The power and goodness of their God becomes manifest in the Exodus experience and then in the experience of Sinai.

To give glory to God means to recognize the divinity of God and in particular to see God's saving presence. God is good and God is powerful. God protects and hovers over Israel. God will assist Israel because of God's glory (Ps 79:9). Since divinity, the power and goodness of God, endures forever, Israel can be confident that the protecting God will shelter them forever. Israel is created by the glory of God in the Exodus and for the glory of God (Isa 43:7). In this sense the psalmist prays that a people will see the glory of God. "The heavens proclaim his justice and all peoples see his glory" (Ps 97:6).

Creativity in God

Ancient peoples had many gods and goddesses. Each had his or her own function in regard to human life with expectations demanded for services rendered. Monotheism developed slowly in the ancient world. Many think that even in the religion of Israel the creed, "Hear O Israel your God is one," need not necessarily refer to monotheism but rather to the superiority of the Gods of Israel over all other gods. Usually the goddesses in the Ancient Near East fulfilled the creative and spontaneous function of divinity while the male gods existed as the stable and often static principles. When Israel developed clear monotheism, some way had to be found to accommodate the spontaneous and creative principles needed for human life. The ancient authors and teachers solved this problem by speaking of the Spirit of God *(ruah),* the word of

God *(dahbar)*, the wisdom of God *(hokmah)*, and finally, *torah*, the instruction of God.

Over the centuries volumes have been written about these qualities or attributes associated with the God of the Bible. Each attribute functions as an effort to bridge the gap between a transcendent God and a God present in human history and actually accomplishing something. The Spirit *(ruah)* hovers over the waters in Genesis 1:1. In Hebrew the word can also be translated by wind or moving air or even breath. Spirit controls *tohu we bohu* in Genesis and gives new life in Genesis 2:7. The Spirit enters into the prophets and they become the messengers of the Word of God. The Spirit gives life as the presence of God in both human history and in particular human beings.

Word *(dahbar)* is creative and accomplishes what it proposes:

> For as the rain and the snow come down from heaven,
>   and return not until they have watered the earth,
> making it bring forth and sprout,
>   giving seed to the sower and bread to the eater,
> so shall my word be that goes forth from my mouth;
>   it shall not return to me empty,
> but shall accomplish that which I purpose,
>   and prosper in the thing for which I sent it.
>   (Isa 55:10–11)

The word of God reflects a dynamism rooted in the personality of the one who speaks. The word releases a psychic energy and when uttered with power it posits the reality that it signifies. When God thus speaks, the power of God accomplishes what God desires. God speaks and the world comes into existence: "And God said... (Gen 1:3–26). The dynamic reality of the Word brings with it a dianoetic quality. Where English uses *thing* or *deed*, Hebrew uses *Word*. The Bible associates the Word of God more frequently with the prophets. In the mouth of the prophet the dynamic reality of God takes form as an expansion of the living personality of God with the power of God present in what the prophet says. God exercises a creative and dynamic quality through the Word, especially as spoken through the prophets (Fretheim, 1992: 961–68).

If *dahbar* belongs to the prophets, *torah* (instruction or law) belongs to the priests. Frequently translators to English from Hebrew translate *torah* as law. Although not accepted by all scholars, the word probably comes from the word *yarah,* which means to toss, or throw, and was associated with lots. Originally *torah* then was associated with oracles (revealed by lot). Thus *torah* involves a divine response to something and since usually in the Ancient Near East the priests gave the divine responses, however obtained, *torah* can better be translated by instruction. More precisely, *torah* means the revelation by God to the people of Israel giving instruction regarding worship and moral behavior. *Torah* teaches the values and the virtues upon which all human behavior should depend. *Torah* as divine instruction can be found throughout the Bible (Isa 8:20; Jer 2:8; 18:18; Amos 2:4).

Wisdom *(hokmah)* implies the ability to discover the order which God has implanted in the universe (von Rad: 74–96). Wisdom helps people learn what works and what does not work. Wisdom consists of maxims and how to conduct oneself in speech and deportment in such a way as to please others, to advance one's success, and to live free from anxiety arising from hostility, opposition, and failure. Like the other qualities of God, wisdom is practical, helping people to live a proper and happy life. It designates the skill of a craftsman (Exod 31:6; 35:10; 1 Kgs 7:14; Isa 40:20). People display wisdom in fulfilling an office or responsibility with the prudence of an effective leader (Deut 1:13, 15; 34:9). Judges should render a decision based on wisdom (1 Kgs 3:28). While learned from observation and tradition, ultimately wisdom is God's gift displayed in creation and recognized by people whom God has blessed to discover its presence.

The God and Father of Jesus Christ

The ancient peoples did not have abstract notions of divinity. Divinity meant something practical and concrete. The divinity of

God connoted God's power and goodness. This understanding becomes evident in the above qualities attributed to God in the Old Testament, *hesed* and *emeth*. God wills to save. The saving presence of God permeates the Old Testament and continues into the New Testament. God remains kind and compassionate and a faithful God, always seeing the goodness in the chosen people and always forgiving. This God Jesus manifests in his living and in his dying. The goodness of the heart of God gives rise to the compassion and kindness and mercy experienced in the ministry of Jesus. Through the encounter with Jesus of these divine virtues, people come to recognize God's glory: "And the Word became flesh and dwelt among us, full of grace *(hesed)* and truth *(emeth);* we have beheld his glory, glory as of the only son from the Father (John 1:14). The Spirit of God, the Word of God, and the Wisdom of God all join instruction to give a practical presence of God in human life in Jesus of Nazareth, offering guidance, direction, inspiration, and support— to discover the true meaning of life both for the individual and the community. To this one God, Abraham, Moses, David, Isaiah, and Jeremiah responded in the Old Testament. This same God Jesus calls "Abba." John the Baptist and the followers of Jesus, especially, Paul and Peter and the Beloved Disciple, recognize the presence of this God in Jesus. Judas has the opportunity but does not respond. Sometimes people wrongly think of the God of the Old Testament as different from the God of the New Testament. Nothing could be further from the truth. All that is said of God from the teachings of the Old Testament finds fulfillment in the teaching and ministry of Jesus. In Jesus, Christians see their God made visible. "Philip, he who has seen me has seen the Father" (John 14:9). "And he who sees me sees him who sent me" (John 12:45). The God of the covenant establishes a new covenant through Jesus: "...this is my blood of the new covenant which is poured out for many for the forgiveness of sins" (Matt 26:28). Kindness, compassion, mercy, and fidelity characterize the life of Jesus. The one God of history enters into history in the birth of Jesus of Nazareth and people of faith recognize the God of Abraham, Isaac, and Jacob.

Conclusion

The Bible knows a God who is near and yet far off, who reveals in the history of Israel and in Jesus, and who also hides in both. The Bible depicts God as humanly comprehensible, often making God like another man, both menacing and unpredictable, judging and forgiving, sometimes in one form and sometimes another. And the Bible depicts God as completely incomprehensible. Yet in these images of God the human race experiences life itself, and in such complexity actually also experiences God. The men depicted in this work relate to this incomprehensible/comprehensible God in many differing ways. Each man has faults with some having greater faults than others. Each has a story to tell. Apart from Jesus himself, sins abound and virtues abound, even in the very sinful David. The stories offer guidance to a world often confused about what is right and what is wrong. The successes and failures give encouragement to individuals bent under the burdens of ordinary life. The God of the Bible participates in human life through chosen people who tell their stories in both the Old Testament and the New Testament.

Topics for Discussion

1. What does God mean to you?

2. If all are created in the image of God, does this mean that all people are equal? Yes or no? How or how not?

3. God chooses whomever God wants. Does this make God unfair?

4. The threefold call to be a sign of salvation, offer the true worship, and care for the poor continue in Christianity. What do they mean to you?

5. Everyone fails in election and in responsibility. What difference does this make in the relationship to God?

6. What does covenant mean to you? Has your idea changed in the study of covenant in the Bible?

7. Why are the covenantal virtues so important in life?

8. The glory of God is the manifestation of power and goodness. Do you think people manifest the glory of God?

Works Consulted

Armstrong, Karen. *A History of God*. New York: Knopf, 1994.

Boadt, Lawrence. *Reading the Old Testament: An Introduction*. New York/Mahwah, NJ: Paulist Press, 1984.

Bright, John. *A History of Israel*. Philadelphia: Westminster Press, 1981.

Brueggemann, Walter. *Theology of the Old Testament*. Minneapolis: Fortress Press, 1997.

Fretheim, Terence. *Exodus*. Louisville, KY: John Knox, 1991.

———. "Word of God," *The Anchor Bible Dictionary*. New York: Doubleday, 1992, 961–68.

McKenzie, John L. *Dictionary of the Bible*. Milwaukee, WI: Bruce, 1965, 267–901.

Mendenhall, George, and Gary Herion. "Covenant," *The Anchor Bible Dictionary*, vol. 1. New York: Doubleday, 1992, 1179–202.

Rad, Gerhard von. *Wisdom in Israel*. Nashville, TN: Abingdon, 1972.

Zobel, H. J. "Hesed," *Theological Dictionary of the Old Testament*. Grand Rapids, MI: Eerdmans, 1986, 44–64.

PART I

Men in the Pre-Historical Period of Genesis

The first eleven chapters are often referred to as the pre-historical period of Israel. Some will also consider the stories of the patriarchs as pre-historical. Nothing is historically known with certainty about the origin of the human race. Scientists today think in terms of millions of years when trying to decipher human origins. The Bible teaches neither creationism nor evolution, but rather tells a story about a man and a woman. The history of this period of human origins lies beyond the Bible. The stories of Abraham, Isaac, and Jacob and their progeny also should not be accepted as accurate history. Often legends develop to explain present circumstances or to give legitimacy to individuals and groups functioning in some position of authority. The stories come from a period separated in time often by centuries from the supposed events. This of course causes some problems when historians try to sort out fact from fiction.

No effort will be made to establish with certainty the historicity of the characters depicted in this period. Pay attention to the story rather than the intricacies of the historical interplay between the storyteller and the narrative. In this way, the Bible continues its function in offering guidance to people of all time periods.

Some scholars will also include Moses and the story of the Exodus in this pre-historical period. No doubt with the retelling of the story of the journey from Egypt hyperbole flourishes. This should not detract from the meaning of the story itself. If Moses did not exist, someone would have to invent him to explain Israelitic history. As will become evident, the various narratives attempt to explain the complex relationship between a particular God and a particular people.

The story of Adam and Eve functions more as a parable in which the individual reader views the story as a window to see some aspect of life, and then the parable becomes a mirror in which the individual sees himself or herself, and finally the story becomes a window again in which the reader sees life differently.

Abraham seems more legend than history but perhaps some kernel of history sets the foundation for the stories about him. The use of specific names might give some hint at history. This will be explained later.

Most people think of Moses as the father of Judaism. In fact, Judaism developed more with Ezra and Nehemiah after the exile than with Moses. Yet, without Moses and the Exodus in which God showed power and goodness, surely Judaism would never have developed as the foundation on which Ezra and Nehemiah built.

In each chapter pay attention to the story told about Adam, Abraham, and Moses. The level of history present will vary and in each story the reader will understand something about human life, recognize the self, and then perhaps see life differently.

Chapter One

Adam and Eve

Then God said let us make man *(adham)* in our image
(selem) and after our likeness *(demuth)*.... (Gen 1:26)

For the first time the Bible uses the word *man,* which can
mean the proper name *Adam,* or a collective singular such as
mankind or *humankind,* or as a plural in English, *men.* It can also
be used of individuals, for example in passages using *blessed,* such
as in Psalm 32:2 or Proverbs 28:17, and sometimes functions
adjectivally as *human,* or even indefinitely as *someone* (Wallace:
62). The word never appears in the plural. With such a variety of
meanings in the Hebrew, no wonder confusion exists in translations into English.

The Old Testament uses the word *ahdam* frequently for
humanity or *human being.* The word also clearly expresses the
proper name for the first of the forefathers of the human race in
1 Chronicles 1:1, and the same seems true for Hosea 6:7. Job
31:33 and Deuteronomy 4:32 seem to refer rather to *human being.*
This adds to the confusion. (In this chapter, *ahdam* will be used for
the generic term and *Adam* for the first male.)

19

Ancient Languages

Comments on the meaning of words may appear to be a strange way to begin a study of the first man mentioned in the Bible, but evidently limiting the translation *ahdam* to *man* or to *Adam* or to *male* does not convey the full meaning of the word. The meaning becomes more complicated when compared with the older Semitic language, Akkadian which, while not using *ahdam*, has similar words: *adamatu* meaning dark red soil, and *adamu* meaning red blood (Wallace: 62). The Akkadian word equivalent to *ahdam* is *awilum*, designating the individual as representing the class, usually a full male citizen with legal status as free, in contrast to the deities and animals. The Akkadian traditions about the origin of man are not always uniform. Some have *awilum* created from the blood of a slain god. The Old Babylonian myth of Atrahasis has the blood of a god mixed with clay to form humans (Clifford: 74–82). Other statements concerning the origin of the human race merely mention creation from clay with life or breath given to the clay from the gods.

Scholars differ on the origin of the Hebrew word *ahdam* (Maass: 79–87): The most plausible origin associates *ahdam* with "being red," and thus related to the Akkadian *adamatu* and with the Akkadian myth of the first human created from the earth mixed with the blood of a dead god. This fits in with the general biblical tradition of the creation of the first man from the earth. But then God breathes life into *adam* (Gen 2:7), differing from the origin of man from the mixture of earth and the blood of a slain god. In Genesis God also gives commands and prohibitions, has *adam* name the animals, and from *adam* comes *woman* (Gen 2:15–23).

Whatever the origin of the word *adham* in the Old Testament, in the first chapter of Genesis *ahdam* holds a unique position among all other creatures. To *ahdam*, the human being, God offers commands following the profession that *ahdam* has been created in the image *(selem)* and likeness *(demut)* of God (Gen

1:26). The image of God connotes the position of *ahdam* taking the place of God in creation as a vice-gerent *(selem)*, acting in creation as God would act. *Demut* refers to the creative principle, which God shares with *ahdam* (Vogels: 3–7). Thus far no differentiation of sexes exists in the Old Testament, although some hint can be found in God's remark: "…let *them* have dominion…" (Gen 1:26). "So God created *ahdam* in his own image, in the image of God he created him, male and female he created them" (Gen 1:27). In this verse as well as in Genesis 1:1 the author uses the Hebrew word *bara* which is usually translated as *create*, or sometimes as *made*. Actually Genesis 1:1 can best be understood as God ordering all things from chaos (Fantino; Bernhardt: 245). The differentiation of the sexes follows explicitly in chapter 2. In the opening chapter *ahdam* refers not to *Adam* the first male, but to *ahdam* the first human.

Adam the First Male

Chapter 2 adds an additional understanding of *ahdam* and here the reference clearly refers to Adam the first male: "…there was no man to till the ground" (Gen 2:5). At first reading this could refer to a human being but in context it appears to refer to a male. Since the majority of scholars claim that the second chapter comes from around the time of David (Brueggemann), the normal task of the male at the period was to tend the soil. This reference to a male is also supported by the creation of woman in Genesis 2:21–25.

The use of *adham* in chapter 1 does not make any reference to the creation of *adham* from the earth but the very choice of the word implies such an origin. Chapter 2 makes explicit what was implicit in chapter 1. "…God formed man of dust from the ground, and breathed into him the breath of life; and man became a living being" (2:7). Created from the earth and given the breath of life makes a human a human. Here the combination of earth and breath makes Adam a male human being. Earlier people knew through experience that when a person breathes, the person lives. When a person stops breathing, or when the blood runs out of a person, the person dies. Both breath and blood constitute the fundamental elements for life.

To this man God gives the command to till the garden and keep it (2:15) and prohibits eating of the tree of good and evil (2:17). Before the creation of Eve, the author tells the additional episode of naming the animals. In the ancient world to know a person's name was to know the person, not only what a person does but also who a person is. Such knowledge also gives some control over the other. When Adam names the animals he demonstrates his ability to know the meaning of the different animals and to exercise control over them.

Eve

Although this book proposes to tell the story of men in the Bible, the story of Adam can never be separated from the story of Eve. The creation of woman follows these commands and prohibitions. The etymology of Eve, a proper name given by Adam, remains uncertain (Wallace, "Eve": 676–77). Genesis gives an explanation of Eve as the mother of all living (3:20). The word may come from the Akkadian and perhaps is related to the Akkadian goddess Ashereh as the mother goddess. Ashereh also includes in her ritual the serpent and fertility and even a sacred tree. In the ancient story, life and fertility follow the worship of Ashereh (Wallace, "Eve": 677).

Dependence and Responsibility

God created both Adam and Eve in the divine likeness. They together will have dominion, act in the place of God in creation, be creative, and obey the commands and prohibitions. These three chapters of Genesis declare human dependence upon God. Life exists personally between birth and death and all flows from the power of God alone.

Along with dependence comes responsibility. Adam and Eve must obey the will of God both positively, what to do, and negatively, what not to do. Chapter 3 of Genesis tells the story of Adam and Eve in the garden and demonstrates the movement away from the ancient relation between people and God: from loving obedience and acting as the children of God, to self-interest and exploitation of self, each other, and even of the earth.

The Story of Adam and Eve

The majority of scholars historically situate the second and third chapters of Genesis in the time of David. Even those who date it much later place the origin of the chapters in the court. Whether David or another king, any king would fit Adam and Adam would fit any king. Kings like to decide for themselves what is right and wrong. Most people like to follow their example. People prefer to decide what is right and wrong for themselves. Unfortunately, this does not work. The serpent promises Eve to be like God, "knowing good and evil," and Eve falls into the trap. If David is the real Adam, he easily fell into the trap of deciding for himself what is right or wrong throughout his life. David wanted an empire and did whatever he needed to do to get it. He also wanted women and even took a married woman to bed. Of course, deciding for oneself what is right or wrong brings problems and even death. Adam and Eve learned that soon enough (Brueggemann).

Individuals can make decisions about right and wrong only after at least considering other people. Eve had no such compunction. She wanted the fruit and took it. Adam followed the example of his wife and their eyes were opened and they knew they were naked. Moral decisions always involve other people and in a religious context also involve God. Spouses usually include the other spouse in decision-making. People's deciding for themselves what is right or wrong brings havoc into society and destroys relationships (L'Heureux: 67–71). Genesis 2–3 teaches precisely the destruction of those relationships.

Wrecked Harmony

Before the decision to eat the fruit, Adam and Eve lived as companions in harmony with God and with the earth. Following their decision, this harmony lay fractured on the ground. They hid from God in fear (Gen 3:10); their personal relationship was affected, especially with regard to sexuality (Gen 3:7), and even the earth withdrew its pleasant presence (Gen 3:17–19). People cannot survive if each person thinks that he or she can decide individually what is right or wrong. Moral decisions demand the acceptance of the other, including the other that is God.

Following the failure of Adam and Eve to obey, God condemns the serpent, pronouncing enmity between the woman and the serpent which will remain a continual struggle. The woman will suffer in childbirth, yet will desire her husband but must be subordinate to him. The man suffers as well in his efforts to wrest a living from the earth, until the man returns from whence he came, the earth (Gen 3:8–19).

The second and third chapters of Genesis, by telling the story of Adam and Eve, actually tells the human tale of the temptation for individuals to want to personally decide what is right and wrong. Genesis teaches such a temptation leads to disasters. David knew the disasters and perhaps he recognized himself in the story. People today also have experienced the consequences of such temptation and perhaps they can see themselves in the story of Adam and Eve. The ancient author had a good sense of human psychology and human desire. These chapters function as a mirror not only to the court of David but also to succeeding generations. The mirror reflects contemporary society as well as society a thousand years before Christ.

The Snake

But there is a snake. What about this creature and what role did the serpent play in the story? Returning to the time and court of David offers some possible explanations for the serpent. If David and his court as individuals wanted to decide for themselves right and wrong, the society had a great temptation to follow false gods. Living in the midst of pagans, with pagan rituals and liturgies involving fertility rites, created an opportunity to allow false gods into the worship of the God of Israel and into the life of the community (L'Heureux: 71–72; McKenzie: 113–25). If one had to choose between participating in fertility rites, which included ritual sexual activity and offering incense and animals in sacrifice, humans easily chose the former. Excitement and pleasure in liturgy usually wins over the sacrifice of the heart.

False Gods

The serpent represents the false god of the Canaanites who promised life through its fertility rites. Actually, worshipping false gods brings death. The interpretation of the serpent as the devil loses much in understanding the meaning of the story. Often in the history of biblical interpretation the devil became the source for evil and the destruction of people by people. In fact, the human and personal decision to decide for oneself what is good or bad causes moral evil and the destruction of people—not the devil.

False gods will always compete with the woman but will never triumph over her. The ancient author clearly blames the woman as first introducing evil into the world rather than the man, but then goes on to tell about a struggle that never finishes in victory over the woman. Men and women historically have worshipped false gods, but in the mind of the author of Genesis women failed more in this false worship than men. The truth of this belief, however, may lie more in the society than in reality. People like to blame others rather than accept responsibility.

Adam, the wimp, blames his wife who in turn blames the snake. Both fail, but since the author of Genesis was probably a man he lays more blame on the woman than on the man. At least he has the good sense to acknowledge that the serpent never conquers the woman completely.

The Origin of Moral Evil

Some see the story of Genesis as an effort to explain the origin of moral evil based on an analysis of what happened at the time. During the reign of David the two principal temptations were worshipping false gods and failing to consider God and others in moral decisions. If such was the case at the court of David, in all probability such has always been the case and always will be the same (Rahner: 36–44). The mirror lifted up to reflect David and his court also reflects people today. Extreme self-autonomy, the worship of the false gods of money or power or sex, or a hundred other little false gods, and the failure to accept personal responsibility for one's actions characterizes people of the twenty-first century as it characterized the people of a thousand years before Christ. Much has changed but much has not changed.

Adam the Role Model?

The first man in the Bible does not offer much of a role model. Adam is weak and easily manipulated. He tries to blame Eve for his personal decision and sheepishly hides from God when he knows he has done wrong. Much had been given to Adam: being created in the image and likeness of God, given power over the animals and responsibility for the land. He failed and failed miserably. Adam jumps out of the pages of Genesis as a tragic failure. In the rest of Genesis Adam does little more than generate children. In chapter 4, Eve conceives through Adam and gives birth to Cain, and shortly after, Abel. In 4:25 Adam again "knew" Eve, and Seth was born. Chapter 5 comes from a duplicate source and merely narrates that Adam became a father again in his old age. Adam lived nine hundred and thirty years and then died. In all this time he did nothing more than generate children. The blessing he passed on, however, was a son created in the image and likeness of Adam (5:3). Since Genesis presents Adam as created in the image and likeness of God, then the children of Adam also were created in the image and likeness of God. In many ways, no greater blessing could have been passed on from one generation to another.

Adam in the Old Testament

The rest of the Old Testament pays little attention to Adam. First Chronicles 1:1 refers to Adam in a list of ancestors. Job 31:33 may refer to Adam but also may refer to the generic *man*. Sirach 17:1 refers to man made from the earth and 49:16 shows both uses: the first refers to humankind and the second refers to Adam. Tobit 8:5–7 quotes Genesis 2:18. Wisdom 2:23 refers to Genesis 1:27 and then refers to death coming into the world through the devil, which contains some reference to the serpent in Genesis 3. Wisdom 9:2 refers to Genesis 1 and dominion and Wisdom 10:1 refers to the first formed father of the world. With such an important story, it seems strange that Adam and Eve figure so infrequently in the Old Testament. Eve does not appear at all outside of Genesis 3–4.

Adam and Eve in the New Testament

The New Testament makes more mention of Adam than the Old Testament and also has two references to Eve, in 2 Corinthians 11:3 and 1 Timothy 2:13. The only reference in the gospels to Adam can be found in Luke 3:38 in the genealogy of Jesus. Paul makes the principal references to Adam in Romans 5:14, 1 Corinthians 15:22 and 45 and in deutero-Pauline 1 Timothy 2:13–14. In Romans and Corinthians Paul develops his Adam/Christ typology. In Romans

Paul compares Adam, the one through whom sin and condemnation and death came into the world, to Christ, the one through whom God offered life to the world. Grace and righteousness from Christ confronts sin and death from Adam and overcomes it.

In Corinthians Paul teaches that resurrection comes from Christ. In Adam all died and in Christ all live. The same theme continues in verses 45–49. No doubt, for Paul, Adam was a male and a historical figure. Otherwise the typology would not be true. All humanity has a body in common with Adam, and Paul's readers have the spiritual body in common with Christ.

Jude 14 refers to Adam as the first generation of humanity, and 1 Timothy denies a teaching role to women since Eve was formed after Adam and was deceived and became a transgressor (1 Tim 2:12–14). The author of Timothy, however, offers salvation to women by bearing children (1 Tim 2:15). So much for Adam and Eve in the New Testament.

Conclusion

Whatever one may say about Adam and Eve today, neither the Old Testament nor the New Testament pay great attention to them. In any case, neither comes out very strong with Adam depicted as the weaker of the sexes even in Timothy. After all, Adam merely followed the suggestion of Eve. The contrast with Christ also depicts Adam as bringing grief. The Bible has little good to say about Adam as an individual male. The meaning of *ahdam* as male and female created in the image of God, however, remains a cornerstone of both Jewish and Christian theology. This, of course, remains God's gift, with neither Adam nor Eve having any contribution to make to their blessedness as being "created in the image and likeness of God." Far from being a story of human origins involving creationism, the story of Adam and Eve persists as a powerful warning to people of all ages to be careful of worshipping false gods and never to think that one individual can decide for himself or herself what is right and what is wrong.

Topics for Discussion

1. What did you know (what did people tell you) about Adam and Eve?
    Historical characters?
    Symbolic story?
    Origin of the human race?
    Cause of sin in the world?
    Related to Ancient Near Eastern stories?

2. What did you know (what did people tell you) about:
    The creation of the world?
    God creating everything from nothing?
    How it took six days?
    The difference between the two creation accounts?
    The origin of the human race being from one couple, or many?
    Evolution and creationism?

3. What do scholars teach about these questions now?

4. What do you think about these questions now?

Works Consulted

Bailey, J. A. "Initiation and Primal Woman in Gilgamesh Epic and Genesis 2–3." *Journal of Biblical Literature* 89 (1970): 137–50.

Bernhardt, Karl-Heinz. "Bara," *Theological Dictionary of the Old Testament,* vol. II. Grand Rapids, MI: Eerdmans, 1975, 245.

Brueggemann, Walter. "David and His Theologian." *Catholic Biblical Quarterly* 30 (1968): 156–81.

Clifford, Richard. *Creation Accounts in the Ancient Near East and in the Bible.* Washington, DC: Catholic Biblical Association, 1994.

Fantino, Jacques. "Whence the Teaching *ex nihilo*?" *Theology Digest* 46 (1999): 133–40.

L'Heureux, Conrad. *In and Out of Paradise.* New York: Paulist Press, 1983.

Maass, Fritz. "Adham," *Theological Dictionary of the Old Testament,* vol. I. Grand Rapids, MI: Eerdmans, 1974, 75–87.

McKenzie, John L. *The Two-Edged Sword.* New York: Doubleday, 1966, 113–25.

Rahner, Karl. *Hominisation.* New York: Herder and Herder, 1965, 36–44.

Vogels, Walter. "The Human Person in the Image of God." *Theology Digest* 43 (1996): 3–7.

Wallace, Howard. "Adam," *The Anchor Bible Dictionary,* vol. 1. New York: Doubleday, 1992, 62–64.

———. "Eve," *The Anchor Bible Dictionary,* vol. 2. New York: Doubleday, 1992, 676–77.

Wolff, H. W. "The Kerygma of the Yahwist." *Interpretation* 20 (1966): 131–58.

Chapter Two

Abraham

God called Abraham to give up his past when Abraham moved from Ur of the Chaldeans to Haran:

> Now the LORD said to Abram, "Go from your country and your kindred and your father's house to the land I will show you." (Gen 12:1)

God asked Abraham to give up his future when God said to him:

> "Take your son, your only son Isaac, whom you love, and go to the land of Moriah and offer him there as a burnt offering upon one of the mountains of which I shall tell you." (Gen 22:2)

Abram (the father is exalted), Abraham (the father of a multitude) did both and God "reckoned to him as righteousness" (Gen 5:6).

Historicity

Contemporary scholarship has reached no conclusion on the historicity of Abraham. Did he exist or did subsequent generations create his legends to give some foundation for their own history? Are the stories truly ancient coming from the period shortly after the turn of the second millennium before Christ, or do these stories find their origin in the time of David or even postexilic Israel? (McCarter: 1–24). Is the religion of Abraham his religion or that of the narrators of the legends ascribed by them to Abraham? How much history and how much poetry? For many, following Gunkel, "Legend has woven a poetic veil about the historical memories and hidden their outline" (Gunkel: 22). For others, no history founds the stories of Abraham. Perhaps the comment by G. Ernest Wright expresses the response better than most:

> We shall probably never be able to prove that Abram really existed, that he did this or that, said thus and so, but what we can prove is that his life and times, as reflected in the stories about him, fit perfectly within the early second millennium but imperfectly with any later period. (Wright: 40)

Without trying to solve this perplexing question, many can still ask: "Does it make a difference?" Judaism, Christianity, and Islam each refer to Abraham as their patriarch and ancestor. Perhaps some kernel of truth fills the center of the legend, preserved over centuries. Perhaps the legend itself contains the meaning without any historical foundation. The stories remain and the value of Abraham for the three great religions perdures.

Historical Arguments

A chief argument for the existence of Abraham rests on the comparison with the other patriarchs. All of them (Isaac, Jacob, Israel, and Joseph) are eponymous, associated with a group. Abraham alone appears as a personal name. In the ancient world and even today, the invention of ancestors established bonds of kinship necessary for the unity of a community. The Bible also presents Abraham as a founder of religious sites in both northern and southern Israel. By this he can also be a means of uniting northern and southern tribes (McCarter: 22–24). Perhaps his historical existence does not matter. Perhaps it does, at least in the collective memory of ancient peoples who always needed someone in the past to bring about a unity in the present.

God and Abraham

God makes solemn oaths and promises (Brueggemann, 1997: 166–73). God made significant promises to Abraham: land, a multitude of progeny, and that by his descendants all nations will be blessed (Gen 12:2–3; 22:17–18). People need space and place both as individuals and as groups (Brueggemann, 1977). Place gives people freedom to be themselves. Memories create place. Every person needs the freedom and the memories and groups need them as well. Tribes, nationalities, families, even social groups need their own space, and when they live in that space they create memories for themselves and for future generations. God promised Abraham both the land and future generations, and the memories become the stories passed on from generation to generation (Gen 13:14–17).

Ancient civilizations preserved their stories around shrines and usually on a high place. The different variations of the stories of Abraham may well be founded on the origin in different sanctuaries. Eventually these stories were put together, probably first around the sanctuary in Sion and then finally after the exile. Editors during and after the exile combined all the stories about Abraham from the north of Israel and in the south, and because they wished to preserve all of the legends, the contemporary reader will find discrepancies in reading the book of Genesis. In each case the reader must pay attention to what the story intends rather than try to discern any historical kernel of truth.

The Career of Abraham

After God promised Abram land and progeny, he and his wife Sarai (princess) with Lot his nephew journeyed to Canaan as

God had commanded him. Famine forced them to go to Egypt where Abram told Pharaoh that Sarai was his sister to avoid being killed, so that Pharaoh could take her as his wife (Gen 12:11–13). Chapter 20:12 narrates a similar story but now the deception involves a king and the author explains that truly Sarai was his sister. The legends both preserve the fate of the pharaoh and of the king in taking a married woman to be a wife. In all likelihood the second story wants to avoid the possibility of Abram lying and so adds to the legend the story of Sarai being his half sister (Gen 20:12). In both instances Abram endangers future prosperity by allowing another to take his wife. In both stories Abram prospers. The pharaoh gave him riches (Gen 12:16) and the king did likewise (Gen 20:14–16). Abram grew in wealth and possessions, all because of his deceit concerning Sarai his wife.

The story continues in Canaan. Lot and Abraham separated, dividing the land, with Lot taking the luxuriant Jordan valley. This story depicts Abram as generous and anxious to avoid strife, especially within the family. When Lot is captured by foreign invaders, Abram goes to his defense and rescues Lot and recovers his possessions. Shortly after, he meets Melchizedek (king of Justice) living in Salem (city of peace). The king, no doubt hearing of the victories of Abram, goes out to meet him and offer hospitality. Abram on his part shrewdly offers Melchizedek a tenth of his possessions after the king and priest blessed Abram in the name of the God most high (Gen 14:18–20). Having conquered the other kings in the area, Abram obtained an ally in Melchizedek. By this time the wealth of Abram, begun in deceit, had grown considerably and a tenth would assure cooperation in the future. Abram dealt shrewdly as both general and diplomat (Boadt: 142).

The Covenant

Genesis 15 narrates for the first time a ritual associated with a covenant, or in this case the charter that God offers to Abram. The fire passing between the cut-up offerings signified that God had ratified the agreement and the ritual signified that God pledged to fulfill the covenant, or be like the animals offered in sacrifice. Abram did nothing. Again God renewed his commitment to give both land and descendants (Gen 15:18).

God renews the covenant again in chapter 17 and changes the name Abram to Abraham and Sarai to Sarah. He places on Abraham and his descendants the obligation of circumcision as a sign of what God had promised. Here also God promised a son to Sarah and Abraham and they both laughed (Gen 17:17; 18:12). The son was to be named Isaac (God laughed!).

The Family of Abraham

The rest of Genesis contains many other stories about Abraham. He offers hospitality to strangers (Gen 18:1–8); bargains with God (Gen 18:22–33); Sarah gives birth to Isaac (Gen 21); and Abraham willingly attempts to offer his son in sacrifice (Gen 22). Abraham provides for Sarah at her death and buries her at Hebron (Gen 23). He also obtains a wife for Isaac, marries again (Gen 25), and finally dies at 175 years and also is buried in Hebron.

Abraham's grandson Jacob gave his name to Israel and fathered the twelve tribes—rather than Abraham—but still the history in the Bible and Judaism considered Abraham the progenitor of the nation (Exod 2:24; 4:5; 32:13; Isa 29:22; Ezek 33:24; Mic 7:20). The claim to Canaan by Israel rested on the promise to Abraham, and the God worshipped by the Israelites was always the God of Abraham (Exod 3:6; 4:1; 1 Kings 18:36; Ps 47:9). God fulfills the promise of progeny. Not only does Abraham have a son but his son gives birth to a son who will produce the tribes of Israel. To this day, Jews refer to the God of Abraham, Isaac, and Jacob.

Abraham and Hagar

No presentation of Abraham can exclude his relationship to Hagar. In the ancient world the lack of progeny weighed heavily on husbands and wives. The male in particular needed a male heir not only to continue the family but to provide for the tribe. When Sarah did not have children she willingly allowed her servant to act as a surrogate for Abraham (Gen 16:1–4). Jealousy arose between the two women, however, when Hagar conceived, and Sarah insisted that Hagar be sent away. With the intervention of an angel of the Lord, Hagar returned to Abraham and Sarah (Gen 16:7–15) and Ishmael was born. After the birth of Isaac, once again Sarah insisted that Hagar and her son leave the family of Abraham. Abraham agreed and Ishmael was banished (Gen 20:8–21). God continued to protect Hagar and Ishmael. Abraham, on his part, used Hagar when he thought it necessary and dismissed her when he had a son by Sarah. The father of the nation treated Hagar and her son unjustly on the insistence of his wife, Sarah.

Abraham and Isaac

In Abraham's old age, Sarah conceived and gave birth to a son (Gen 21:1–8). Abraham rejoiced for finally he had true progeny who could receive the promise made to Abraham by God. No doubt the parents loved their only son and had thoughts of a happy old age, and that death would cause no concern, knowing that Isaac would continue the line. But then God asked Abraham to give up his future in the sacrifice of Isaac his son (Gen 22:1–14). Without hesitation Abraham prepared for the sacrifice. The intervention of the angel of God prevented the offering and God restored Isaac to his parents. In this period of human history, many civilizations mistakenly offered human sacrifice as the sign of total dependence on the divine. What better offering could be made than that of a child to a god or goddess as a sign of divine sovereignty? But the God of Abraham wanted no such offering. The willingness to offer sufficed. Abraham received God's good pleasure and God renewed the promise of land and prosperity and nations being blessed because Abraham trusted in God and acted as God directed (Gen 22:15–18).

Abraham, God, and Worship

Throughout his career Abraham built shrines and worshipped (Gen 12:7; 13:4, 18) and the God he worshipped was usually referred to as *Yahweh* (Gen 12:8; 13:4). Additional names for God are also found in the Abraham narrative: *Elohim* (the general term for God and in the plural) in Genesis 17:3 and in several other passages; *El Shaddai* (God almighty) occurs in Genesis 17:1; and *Adonai* (sovereign Lord) in Genesis 15:2, 8. The variety of names testifies to the various understandings of God at this time and may also include the continual thought of polytheism in the Ancient Near East. But even with this multiplication of names, it seems that only one God was addressed. Some question the possibility of monotheism at the supposed period of Abraham and look upon such an understanding as retrojection, from a later period, of the belief in one God. The historical and astonishing impact of the monotheism of Akhenaton, the pharaoh in Egypt during the eighteenth dynasty in the fourteenth century before Christ, demonstrates the actual belief in one God. Whether this can be accepted as a belief held an additional five hundred years to the twentieth century before Christ remains a possibility, but perhaps a remote possibility. Much will depend on the actual understanding of religious experience and revelation during this period. Like many of the legends of Abraham, the actual historicity remains disputed (Bright: 98–103).

Abraham also related directly to God without any intermediary—in particular, priests. God spoke to Abraham in visions and even appeared in human form (Gen 18:1–33) accompanied by two angels. Eliezer, the servant of Abraham, spoke of Abraham's faith and God's care for him (Gen 24:27) and God commended Abraham to Abimelech as a prophet (Gen 20:7). The God whom Abraham worshipped was known to him personally and this God explained the purpose of the revelation and the theophanies, even if at times Abraham loses his patience in trying to understand this God.

Abraham trusted in God in the presence of numerous difficulties and God declared him righteous. *Sedaqa* (righteousness) in Hebrew has many aspects but can best be understood as God giving Abraham the right to stand in the presence of God. Abraham did nothing to deserve such a privilege. God declared and the word of God effected the change in the status of Abraham. In Romans Paul recalls this tradition and applies it to anyone who trusts in God through faith in Jesus (Rom 4:3–24).

Conclusion

Asked to give up his past and future, Abraham willingly agrees. God promised him land, posterity, and a great name. Generous with his nephew Lot, he rescues him and shares his wealth. Following the tradition of the Ancient Near East, Abraham offers hospitality to strangers, bargains with God for just people, and takes care of his loyal wife to her death. Like a good father he cares for his son and even provides a wife for Isaac to insure posterity.

The Bible joins to this picture the deceit of Abraham, the use of others for his own gain, his willingness to dismiss Hagar and Ishmael—clearly an unjust decision—and his laughter at the thought of a son in his old age. Abraham surely is not a plastic saint. He has trouble understanding God. He fails in his deceit and in his use of others. He does not always appear as strong in convictions. Abraham seems to be a "plodder" who goes through life blundering with undeserved successes, doing good and accomplishing results in spite of himself. Sometimes life seems like a joke to Abraham. Just when he thinks everything is going well, his world turns upside down. But then quickly it turns right side up and Abraham continues on. He started with a journey and his life in Genesis consists of journeys. God accompanies Abraham and

Abraham appears to be on intimate terms with God. Finally, Abraham puts his life together based on his faith in God. The redeeming feature of Abraham, as depicted in the book of Genesis, remains always his trust, his faith in God.

Topics for Discussion

1. Does history contribute to an understanding of faith? Is historical accuracy always necessary?

2. What do you think of the history in the stories of the patriarchs?

3. Does Abraham appeal to you as a role model? Explain.

4. Can Abraham, the "plodder" in life, help people to live as people of faith?

5. Abraham is the father of Judaism, Christianity, and Islam. What might this mean to some of the problems of the contemporary world situation?

6. Do you trust God enough to give up both past and future?

7. Why is faith more important than religion?

Works Consulted

Boadt, Lawrence. *Reading the Old Testament: An Introduction.* New York/Mahwah, NJ: Paulist Press, 1984.

Bright, John. *The History of Israel.* Philadelphia: Westminster Press, 1981.

Brueggemann, Walter. *The Land.* Philadelphia: Fortress Press, 1977.

———. *Theology of the Old Testament.* Minneapolis: Fortress Press, 1997.

Gunkel, H. *The Legends of Genesis.* New York: Schocken, 1964.

McCarter, P. Kyle. "The Patriarchal Age: Abraham, Isaac, Jacob." In *Ancient Israel,* edited by Hershel Shanks. Englewood Cliffs: Prentice Hall, 1999, 1–32.

Millard, A. R. "Abraham," *The Anchor Bible Dictionary,* vol.1. New York: Doubleday, 1992, 35–41.

Wright, G. Ernest. *Biblical Archeology.* Philadelphia: Westminster Press, 1962.

Chapter Three

Moses

Although the Exodus and Moses have been the subject of art and poetry and motion pictures—and anyone who has even heard of Judaism knows Moses is involved in the Exodus, and most people have wonderful visual images of Moses parting the sea—no non-biblical references offer an account of Moses nor the Exodus event. The book of Exodus refers to 600,000 men, not counting women and children, leaving Egypt (Exod 12:37) along with flocks and herds. With such an unusual event one would think that some record would appear somewhere. The question of historicity rests then solely on the accuracy of the biblical account. To put this into perspective: two rows of fifty men eventually amounting to 600,000, walking side by side ten feet apart to walk comfortably, would require a procession of twelve miles, not counting women and children and flocks and herds. Evidently something has happened over the centuries during which the story has been told. For this reason and many others, scholars and readers of Exodus have questioned the accuracy of the account of the Israelites living in and leaving Egypt.

Of course some think the account is historically accurate, written by Moses himself. In fact for centuries many thought that Moses wrote the first five books of the Bible (Pentateuch). Catholics held this position as late as the beginning of the twentieth century (*Rome and...*: 118). Not until 1948 were Catholic scholars free to study and question exactly how Moses should be related to the Pentateuch (*Rome and...*: 150–53). Presently some few, especially among the Jewish Orthodox, still maintain that Moses actually wrote or dictated the first five books of the Bible. Others accept some historical kernel regarding Moses and the Exodus, and some think that all is legend and cannot be dated earlier than the tenth century before Christ. If the Exodus took place, most scholars place it around 1250 BC.

The Historical Question

Gerhard von Rad, a German, and "one of the most prominent Old Testament scholars of this century" (Blenkinsopp: 16), studied the Exodus and Moses traditions and concluded that one cannot isolate any historical events associated with Moses, nor can one write a tradition of Moses explaining from where the tradition came. Von Rad saw no possibility of discovering the actual course of events. He believed, also, that the Sinai event is a later addition to the story of the settlement in Canaan. And in fact, that all the stories are legends gathered at separate sanctuaries. The Exodus comes from the sanctuary at Gilgal and the Sinai experience from the sanctuary at Sheckem (von Rad: I, 4–8; 291–96). "If we try to determine the age of these traditions we are seldom able to advance beyond very general datings, if we are not in fact altogether in the dark" (von Rad, I, vi).

Another German scholar of the Pentateuch, Martin Noth, isolates five themes in the Pentateuch: the patriarchs, the Exodus event, Sinai, the wanderings in the desert, and the conquest of the land. All originally were oral traditions and Moses "functioned as the editorial bracket binding all the themes together" (Noth: 160–61).

More contemporary scholars such as B. Childs, G. W. Coats, and N. K. Gottwald accept much more historicity in the Moses and Exodus tradition than their predecessors. In various ways each one wants to accept Moses as one who unites the various traditions.

Albright all along maintained that the biblical tradition about Moses "is strongly supported by a rapidly increasing mass of evidence uncovered by archeologists and philogians" (Albright: 120), and John Bright claims, "Over all these events towers the figure of Moses...there can be no doubt that he was, as the Bible portrays him, the great founder of Israel's faith. The events of Exodus and Sinai require a great personality behind them" (Bright: 126–27). For these scholars and others, to deny a role for someone who is called Moses would not only fail to explain the origin of Judaism, but would demand an invention of some one personality to found and mold together so many different experiences and events.

Any conclusion regarding the actual historical figure of Moses rests on possibilities and probabilities. Those who regard the traditions in the Pentateuch as reasonably well founded historically present the probability of most of the events as historical. Those who take a more critical view will accept possibility but not probability. Of course, others accept the traditional understanding of Moses. As in much of the Bible, individual readers may come to their own conclusions concerning history.

The Name *Moses*

The name *Moses,* contrary to popular opinion, expressed in Exodus 2:10, does not mean "to draw out" but means "to give birth." The name *Rameses,* one of the most famous pharaohs, means "Re is born." Thus *Moses* means someone is born with no thought of the actual person. Or, someone related to some god is born. The parents are not named in Exodus 2:1 and later, in Exodus 6:14, the names *Amram* and *Jochebed* are probably artificially created to establish some legitimacy.

Some historical nucleus probably founds the events narrated in the Pentateuch and this would apply to Moses as well. These traditions also probably originated at shrines at high places. The many traditions mentioned by Noth find a unity in the person of Moses as a historical figure. The written composition of legends probably began around the ninth or eighth centuries BCE, with the final editing taking place in the fifth century. The various oral traditions developed at different times and in different places with different forms, all relating to the question of the origins of Israelitic faith. More than that, in the words of von Rad, "remains in the dark." In response to the call of God, Moses led his people from Egypt, helped constitute them as the people of God at Sinai, interceded for them during wanderings, and brought them to Moah where he died.

Background

Almost everyone who knows anything about the Bible knows the story of the birth and childhood of Moses. Most do not know the story of Sargon I of Akkad (c. 2371–2316):

> Call me Sargon; I am the child of a priest and an unknown pilgrim from the mountains. Today I rule an empire from the city of Agade. Because my mother did not want anyone in the city of Asupiranu to know that she had given birth to a child, she left me on the bank of the Euphrates River in a basket woven from rushes and waterproofed with tar. The river carried my basket down to a canal where Akki, the royal gardener, lifted me out of the water and reared me as his own. (Matthews: 85)

Note the parallel. Compare the birth of Moses with the birth of Jesus. An evil king (Pharaoh) tries to destroy Moses at his birth. An evil King (Herod) tries to destroy Jesus at his birth (Matt 2:13–18). In both cases many boys will die, but God sees to it that both Moses and Jesus survive. The stories support both the providence of God and the efforts on the part of evil people to thwart the will of God.

Exodus 2:1 refers to Moses' ancestry as the tribe of Levi. But unlike Aaron, Moses does not always function as a priest. The legends of Moses related him to Levi since he does bring people to God and God to people, the most basic responsibility of a priest. Later tradition wanted Moses to be part of the tribe of Levi because, by then, priests came from this tribe alone.

Efforts to demonstrate Moses' actual Egyptian background seem artificial. Apart from the birth story, Exodus attested to no particular relationship to the Egyptian court, and during the negotiations with Pharaoh no reference to his Egyptian upbringing is made. Nor are the efforts to relate Moses to the monotheism of Akhenaton completely successful (Boadt: 158–59). Possibly some of the thoughts and words of this pharaoh on monotheism remained in the mind of the settlers from the north, but history demonstrates that monotheism began to develop slowly in the ancient world.

The Midian influence on Moses, however, seems strong in the book of Exodus (2:16–4:19). Moses fled to Midian after he killed the Egyptian, met the daughters of Jethro, and married Zipporah. Jethro was a priest of Midian and some see Moses indebted to Jethro for learning of the worship of Yahweh. Whether Yahweh was worshipped before Moses cannot be answered definitively. Many think the worship of Yahweh was known among the Midian clans of the Sinai Peninsula since Jethro was a priest of Midian who offered sacrifice with Moses (Exod 18:10–12). Some relationship exists between the religion of the Israelites and that of Midian (Bright: 127). The worship of one God, Yahweh, developed slowly over many centuries however, and even with the acceptance of Yahweh, as already noted, the Israelitic religion did not always maintain an exclusive monotheism. Whatever the origins of the worship of Yahweh, Moses figures prominently in the development of monotheistic Judaism. Rather than seeing one clean line of development, a gradual development from many strands come together, especially when Moses has his religious experience.

The Religious Experience of Moses

Classical theories of religious experience, whether of William James or Rudolph Otto, fit nicely into the Moses story. James offers four characteristics: ineffable, a noetic quality, the individual remains passive, and the event is transient (James: 299–301). Otto speaks of the *mysterium tremens* and the *mysterium fascinans* (Otto: 12–40). Moses cannot clearly understand or describe his experience; he learns about God and about himself; it happens to him and passes quickly. He experienced both the sense of fear and the sense of fascinating mystery. Thus begins the specific religious traditions associated with Yahweh and Judaism.

The burning bush can be explained in various ways depending on the presence or absence of bias, and depending on how one views the miraculous. In the Sinai Peninsula grow certain bushes with brilliant red flowers. At a particular time of the year, the wind blowing the pollen with the presence of the red color could give the impression from a distance of a burning bush which is not consumed. This could explain what Moses saw. Of course, God also could have worked a miracle. Whatever the explanation, Moses experienced the presence of God and he became a changed man, who then changed the history of the world (Exod 3:1–4:17).

Throughout the experience Moses seems timid and reluctant. He wants to avoid his responsibility by complaining that he is too lowly (Exod 3:11); no one will listen (Exod 4:1); he cannot speak (Exod 4:10), and finally Moses just wants out and asks God to send someone else (Exod 4:13). In each instance God assures Moses he will not be alone; God will be with him. As often happens in the Old Testament, God gets angry at the failure of people to respond (Exod 4:14). Ultimately Moses accepts his mission to the enslaved people and becomes their leader.

The timid and reluctant Moses, however, acts boldly enough to ask the name of God. In the ancient world, to know a person's name was to know the person and to have some power over the person. The earlier chapter dealt with the name of God as *ehyeh asher ehyeh*. The name *Yahweh* can mean "He who causes what is" or "I will be what I will be." When combined with the God of Abraham it also connotes the God who was always present to Israel throughout the history of the people. Ultimately in the Old Testament the name carries with it a sense of creating the people and sustaining them through all of history.

The Mission of Moses

As priest, Moses brings God to the people and the people to God. As leader, Moses brings the enslaved people out of Egypt to freedom. The book of Exodus does not depict Moses as a man of unusual piety. The reason for being at Sinai is unknown. He comes upon the place as a shepherd. God drafted him for the job. Moses did not volunteer. He had his numerous objections but finally acquiesced and began his journey from Egypt to the banks of the Jordan. Gradually he wins the allegiance of the people as he negotiates with Pharaoh (Exod 5:1–11:10). After much resistance the final plague, the loss of the first-born, human and animal (Exod 12:29–32), causes Pharaoh to insist that Moses lead the people out of Egypt.

Over the years many interpretations have been given to the phrase "Let my people go" (Exod 9:1). Martin Luther King used the phrase in the civil rights movement of the sixties. Liberation Theology used it in the quest for freedom from social and political and economic oppression in Latin America. The feminist movement and the gay movement also have used it as a battle cry. Each has been an accommodated use of the Bible. Moses requested freedom not to leave Egypt but to be free to worship God (Exod 10:24). Reading the story in Exodus carefully supports this view since Pharaoh wanted the people to go without taking along flocks and herds (Exod 10:24). It seems Pharaoh planned to give permission to leave and then return. Moses objects and wants to take all the possessions and Pharaoh gives in (Exod 10:28). In these chapters, doublets and confusion abound. The differing accounts of going and not going can be attributed to the various traditions from different times and places concerning Moses. Originally Moses probably wanted to lead the people to the desert to worship God. The people "borrowed" jewelry and other things of value (Exod 11:2). They went into the desert, and when they did not return the army of Pharaoh went after them and experienced some disaster. The Bible clearly states what happened to the army of Pharaoh (Exod 14:26–31): they drowned in the closing waters. Like many tales from the Ancient Near East, what actually happened is covered with centuries of storytelling. The following is probably one of the oldest verses in the Old Testament:

> I will sing to the LORD for he has triumphed gloriously;
> the horse and his rider he has thrown into the sea. (Exod 15:1b)

God saved Israel and the Egyptians suffered, and God used the waters to accomplish what God had intended. Beyond that, all is speculation. Some think that the ordinary marshy land which becomes dry during part of the year allowed the Israelites to cross. By the time the Egyptians arrived on the scene the ordinary spring rains had begun and the army drowned, with the chariots mired in the mud, and then suddenly a flash flood enveloped them. Whatever the truth, the miracle was the preservation of Israel.

Some think that behind this composite picture lies two separate accounts: an Exodus led by Moses, and another account narrating an expulsion after the death of the first born (de Vaux: 373). The unclear account on the actual Exodus with its timing and motivation points to several traditions coming together to combine human efforts with the divine assistance. In the end the Bible preserves a belief in divine providence and human folly.

The Passover

During the Exodus narrative explaining the actual leaving of Egypt, the author of Exodus interrupts the drama with directives for the celebration of the Passover meal (chapter 12). These descriptions, however, come more from the peaceful celebration of the events surrounding the leaving of Egypt long after the actual period. The ritual includes eating certain food in a standing position and prayers chosen to emphasize the sufferings of the ancestors as they fled in fear of Pharaoh, with trust in their God.

The feast probably combines two ancient liturgical festivals. In the first feast, shepherds celebrated by killing a newborn lamb in the spring and sprinkling the blood to drive off evil spirits as the tribe moved to the new springtime pastureland. In the second feast, farmers celebrated by removing the yeast and old grain to celebrate the new life begun in spring. The feasts were combined to celebrate the new life of God's people by warding off any dangers to human life. These feasts the Israelites combined with the Exodus event to be commemorated each year in the springtime.

Sinai

No one can doubt that the dominant event during the wanderings in the desert took place at Sinai. The actual narrative (chapter 19 to chapter 24) combines many sources and traditions. Above all, the religious experience at Sinai by Moses and the people binds God's covenant with Israel forever through Moses with the Exodus event.

Throughout the wanderings the people murmured against God and Moses, with both God and Moses growing angry with the complaints. During the Sinai experience Moses acts both as God's representative to the people as the lawgiver, and the people's representative to God as intercessor. Eventually both Moses and God overlook their anger and the people become the special people of God with Moses as the leader. Much has already been said regarding covenant, and in particular the Mosaic covenant. Although often presented as bilateral, in the history of Israel God always relents and forgives the people. Once God chose Israel,

God never reneged on that relationship in spite of any failures on the part of the people.

The Death of Moses

Why did God prevent the faithful servant Moses from entering into the promised land? Both Deuteronomy 3:23–27 and 24, and Numbers 20:12, 27:12 speak of the death of Moses. Did Moses commit some sin which prevented him from entering the promised land? Was the sin theological? Some see the sin in the story of the scouts and the rebellion in Numbers 13–14, or the lack of faith at Meribah (Num 20:13). The Bible does not clearly explain. Perhaps the heroic tradition surrounding Moses and the mighty deeds of God allows the hero to suffer for the people throughout his life up to and including the failure to lead the people into the promised land. Moses, like the Servant in Second Isaiah, takes upon himself the sins of the people and personally suffers the pain of never fulfilling his hope to reach the promised land. And so, the burial place of Moses remains unknown.

Moses in the Bible

Apart from the Pentateuch, Moses appears more than 120 times in the Old Testament. Surprisingly, however, the name occurs in the prophets only 17 times. In the New Testament Matthew mentions Moses 6 times, even while presenting Jesus as a new Moses figure. Mark mentions him 8 times, Luke 10 times. By far the Gospel which more frequently takes up the theology of Moses is John's Gospel, mentioning him 12 times and in rather important sections of the Gospel. The Acts of the Apostles mentions Moses 19 times, which can easily be understood as the early church attempted to assure Jewish Christians of the roots of the Jesus tradition in the Old Testament. Paul speaks of Moses 9 times in the authentic letters. Hebrews mentions Moses 10 times, again understandable in the author's attempt to prove the superiority of the sacrifice of Jesus over all Old Testament sacrifices and rituals, including the priesthood.

The Real Moses

Attempting to separate fact from fiction and history from legend leaves any reader of the Bible in a quandary. Better to avoid the attempt. The Bible presents Moses as an unlikely leader and prophet. He was both timid and bold in his relationship with God and with the pharaoh and the people. Moses persevered in following the Word of God even if not always with much enthusiasm. He accepted his role as the instrument of God and creatively fulfilled his mission. Whether a great military leader or not, he brought the people close to the goal. Throughout the period Moses acted as a spiritual guide and even a miracle worker in the minds of many. Frequently he lost his temper with the people given into his charge. Both lawgiver and interpreter of the law, he continued to intercede for the people even after the golden calf (Exod 32–33).

Often Moses related intimately with God and saw the glory of God (Exod 33:17–23). The tradition also preserved his meekness (Num 12:3). Throughout Exodus he functioned as a shepherd for the people and eventually led them to the promised land. Was his great sin a doubt in fulfillment of the Word of God, or did he die the tragic hero failing to experience the fullness of his hopes for himself and for the people? Who can say with certainty? The tragic hero theory appeals precisely because the image appears in both the Old Testament and the New Testament. Saviors usually suffer in their efforts to save.

Founder of Judaism

Most people do not believe that Moses actually wrote the first five books of the Bible. He inspired them and in this sense, as the leader in the Exodus and the intercessor with God, Judaism begins with Moses. Like the prophets in later centuries he pointed out the presence and absence of God in human life. He acted like a priest in offering sacrifice and in giving oracles. While not the founder of the worship of Israel including priesthood and sacrifice, he initiated a relationship to God expressed in ritual. The political and religious institutions of Israel came much later. Judaism developed over many centuries and continues to develop to this day. Moses began the process in his experience of God and his efforts to lead others to have a similar experience. Through him, the people of Israel became the people of God.

As the founder of Judaism, Moses proposed a God who demanded a moral code. He taught belief in a God of history who leads people to their destiny. Moses proclaimed a God who used nature for determined purposes and used humans while remaining independent of them. Moses mediated a covenant which was bilateral and in which God always forgave. The basic understanding of the God of Judaism goes back to Moses and his religious experiences.

Conclusion: Saint Moses

The city of Venice has a church dedicated to Saint Moses. Most Christians do not think of Moses as a saint but surely he was. But like Abraham, Moses was far from a plastic saint. He recognized his own weakness and had his insecurities; yet he persevered in the mission to which God had called him. Eventually he recognized that his mission was more important than his personal life for we know very little about his family. He often seems lonely. In many ways he lived and died like the tragic hero of human experience who gives his life in an effort to give both light and life to others.

Topics for Discussion

1. What about the Exodus appeals to you?

2. Do you like to think of the actual history, or do you pay more attention to the meaning of the story?

3. What do you make of the parallels with Sargon and Jesus?

4. What is your immediate reaction to Moses?

5. After reflection, what do you think of Moses?

6. What are the strengths of Moses in the book of Exodus?

7. Why are Christians interested in Moses? Is he a saint?

Works Consulted

Albright, W. F. *Archeology, Historical Analogy and Early Biblical Tradition*. Baton Rouge, LA, 1966.

Beegle, Dewey. "Moses," *The Anchor Bible Dictionary*. New York: Doubleday, 1992, 909–18.

Blenkinsopp, Joseph. *The Pentateuch*. New York: Doubleday, 1992.

Boadt, Lawrence. *Reading the Old Testament: An Introduction*. New York/Mahwah, NJ: Paulist Press, 1984.

Bright, John. *A History of Israel*. Philadelphia: Westminster Press, 1981.

De Vaux, Roland. *The Early History of Israel*. Philadelphia: Westminster Press, 1978.

James, William. *The Varieties of Religious Experience*. New York: Simon and Schuster, 1997.

Matthews, V. and D. Benjamin. *Old Testament Parallels*. New York/Mahwah, NJ: Paulist Press, 1997.

Noth, Martin. *A History of Pentateuchal Traditions*. Englewood Cliffs, NJ: Prentice Hall, 1972.

Otto, Rudolf. *The Idea of the Holy*. New York: Oxford University Press, 1958.

Rad, Gerhard von. *Old Testament Theology,* vols. I and II. London: Oliver and Boyd, 1967.

Rome and the Study of Scripture. St. Meinrad, IN: Grail, 1962.

PART II

Men in the Historical Period

The historical books of the Old Testament, especially the books of Samuel, Kings, and Chronicles, purport to describe actual people with definite events in a defined period to time and space. The events creating the kingships of Saul, David, and Solomon are especially dear to both Jews and Christians. Anyone who knows the history of the compilation of the books of the Old Testament also knows that the stories were joined together in some coherent manner only after the exile, possibly in the fifth century. What does this do to the actual history of these three kings?

As was true in the prehistorical period, with the passage of time some elements fall out of the story and others become embedded as essential to the history. The differences can often be seen when the same event or character is described in First and Second Samuel and then in Chronicles. Historical accuracy probably lies in the middle, especially when dealing with David. Since some writing of the stories of Israel took place around the time of David, more confidence can be given to his life and character than to the previous studied men in the Bible. This should not, however, eliminate any presence of historical rewriting after the fact. As was true in the study of Adam, Abraham, and Moses, the reader need not become too concerned with historical accuracy. Pay attention to the story.

With Isaiah and Jeremiah history plays a more significant role. The prophets existed in a particular period of history with historical events which can be documented. What they say and what they do make sense only if the reader knows something of what is happening in the Ancient Mid East.

From Assyria to Babylon, 722–587 BCE

The history of Israel from the eighth century before Christ to the destruction of the Temple in Jerusalem in 587 witnessed a succession of political forces that made life very difficult for anyone living in the narrow strip of land bordering the Mediterranean from modern Lebanon to Egypt. Tumultuous change characterized the time and the land. Many of the classical prophets lived and died during this period.

After the death of Solomon the kingdom of David was split into Israel and Judah. For two hundred years the kingdom of David prospered even when split into two independent realms. During this period no great empire existed to cause serious problems for the tribes of Jacob. After the middle of the eighth century, such peace and tranquility never existed again. Assyrians swept down from the north and enveloped the kingdom of Israel. Even if Judah survived for an additional 150 years, that kingdom never had independence again.

Jeroboam, King of Israel, died in 747, and after his death the northern kingdom experienced one disaster after another. Internal corruption facilitated the demise of Israel and within twenty-five years, Israel as a kingdom ceased to exist. In 722 the northern kingdom, the richer and more fertile part of the original kingdom of David, fell to the Assyrians. In 587 the southern kingdom of Judah fell to the Babylonians.

The two books of Kings tell the story from the time of David to the fall of the southern kingdom of Judah. Although separated by almost a century and a half, and further divided by geography, the history of both kingdoms during this period contains the same elements: violence and warfare, political and religious corruption, the oppression of the poor, and above all, the worship of false gods. Both kingdoms, and both leaders and followers, failed in their relationship to the God of their ancestors. In this context of violence and infidelity, the classical prophets appear from Amos to Ezechiel.

Each prophet in the Old Testament has his own personality and particular mission. What binds all of the prophets together is a sense of a divine imperative. They cannot *not* do what God calls them to do. They might at times wish to do otherwise, as evident in Jeremiah, but are unable to avoid the call which God has given them. In every instance they proclaim to all—both leaders, religious and civil, as well as to the people—a need to return to their commitment to the God of Abraham, Isaac, and Jacob. In each instance both leaders and people fail in their attempt to avert disaster and they bring upon themselves the pain and suffering that flows from any misuse of power and neglect of God.

To pick just two prophets from among the many writing prophets may appear far from sufficient. But this work is an introduction to some of the men in the Bible and not an exhaustive treatment of all of them. The first part of Isaiah comes from the period of Assyria and the later sections come from the time of Babylon. Jeremiah comes from the period of the Babylonian war and exile. It's difficult to find a greater contrast in prophets than these two. Isaiah lived as the eternal optimist and Jeremiah not only preached doom and gloom, but also personally lived it. Each prophet can be understood only when the reader understands something of the history behind the words. Each prophet had experienced a divine imperative. Each had met with misunderstanding, rejection, pain, and suffering. Each remained faithful to God and each made a contribution to Israelitic life and to human life in general. Each pointed out both the presence and absence of God, warning that ignoring God's presence multiplies calamities.

Isaiah gets along better with God than Jeremiah. Ultimately, however, each prophet found fulfillment in the living out of his vocation.

Works Consulted

Anderson, Bernhard. *Understanding the Old Testament.* Upper Saddle River, NJ: Prentice Hall, 1998.

Boadt, Lawrence. *Reading the Old Testament: An Introduction.* New York/Mahwah, NJ: Paulist Press, 1984.

Bright, John. *A History of Israel.* Philadelphia: Westminster Press, 1981.

Chapter Four

David

Will the real David stand up? Was David a man who never saw a sin he did not like, or a saint who loved God above all and to whom God repaid the compliment? Saint or sinner or both, it all depends on what one reads in the Old Testament and what constitutes saint or sinner. First and Second Samuel depict David as the flawed hero, more sinner than saint. First Chronicles portrays David as the saint, the beloved, the giant figure in the history of Israel who maintained his prominence well into the New Testament and into Christianity (McCarter, 1986: 117–29).

David fascinates many and angers many. Not too many people hold a neutral opinion when they read the passages in the books of the Old Testament dealing with David. So many nouns describe him: shepherd, musician, poet, warrior, general, king, genius both in politics and in public relations. So many adjectives come to mind when thinking of David: ambitious, self-promoting, cunning, compassionate, faithful, loving, committed, controlling, vengeful, forgiving, angry, sad, bold, silly, humble, proud. So many accomplishments surround his legends: sired a dynasty, centralized leadership, subverted the institutions of judges and prophets, planned a permanent Temple, created a nation, established a federal cult with his own priests, and controlled, controlled, controlled.

Poet and Warrior

Perhaps the best explanation of David's personality lies in the conflicting aspects of his life as poet and warrior. The genius in the military played the harp and wrote poetry. These characteristics do not usually go together. The latter is mystic; the former is practical and utilitarian. The poet enjoys peace and tranquility. The warrior burns with a zeal for conflict and battle and conquest. Often, however, when combined these characteristics strengthen each other. The poet makes the warrior gentler and the warrior makes the poet fiercer. In the end the poet/warrior accomplishes much.

David and Moses

Contrast the above characteristics of David with Moses. The founder of Judaism appears as a reluctant leader, humble and clumsy of tongue, who yielded to a successor of another tribe, engaged in a type of collective leadership, and had a traveling sanctuary with no permanent dwelling for God or for himself. Intimate with God, he never reached his goal as God's messenger and lies in an unknown grave. David lives on as a mighty hero who has a tomb in Jerusalem and a city which is called "David's." Moses lives on as a wimp compared to him. No wonder neutrality has few followers when it comes to David.

The Name *David*

The name *David* appears in the early second millennium before Christ in the Old Babylonian. The name also appears in Moabite in the ninth century before Christ. Some see the name as a throne name meaning *chief,* which seems erroneous. Probably it means *darling* or *beloved* and, knowing David as presented in the Old Testament, who could doubt that he gave himself this name?

More than a thousand times the name appears in the Old Testament, and fifty-nine times in the New Testament. Clearly David dominates more than Moses throughout the Jewish tradition and continues in the Christian tradition. And like Moses, people have trouble separating the fact from the fiction, the history from the legend. All great personages grow in death and often take on a greater significance as the stories are told and retold, especially over centuries. While unable to separate the real David from the stories, no doubt exists that Judaism preserved David as beloved by God. The stories tell much about this relationship between God and God's beloved David.

David and Goliath

Few people do not know the story of David and Goliath. The underdog wins and goes on to become a king. Fairy tales do come true. Second Samuel 21:19, however, has Elhanan killing the giant and everyone knows that David did it for it is recorded in 1 Samuel 17: 41–51. First Chronicles tries to harmonize the account by claiming that Elhanan killed the brother of Goliath. No one can be sure of what happened, but surely something happened in the valley of Elah to bring victory to the Israelites and why not associate it with David? (Bright: 192). Of course, if David did take a throne name, perhaps originally his name was Elhanan, which name implies invoking God. Beloved of God sounds better than evoking God. David would have preferred the latter. Besides, who could ever doubt that David killed Goliath after seeing the statue of David by Michelangelo?

The Family

Like much about David, various stories surround his original family as well as the family he established with his many wives. He is one of at least eight sons of Jesse of Bethlehem (1 Sam 17:12–14) and he had some sisters, although whether full sisters or half sisters is unclear (1 Chr 2:16). The books of Ruth and Chronicles, as well as Matthew and Luke, contain David's ancestry with each tracing him back to Judah. His ancestry was not entirely Jewish, through Ruth the Moabite and Tamar the Canaanite. Rahab, the prostitute of Jericho, is also mentioned but no record of her ancestry exists in the Bible. As a resident of Jericho she could have been Canaanite, but also from one of the Israelitic tribes who lived in Jericho.

As the youngest son of at least eight, David could not have expected any inheritance from his father. In those times younger sons learned a profession to enter into the service of a more powerful and wealthy patron. Perhaps this explains his musical training. Evidently David had other talents since he eventually became a great warrior, and by the time he arrived at Gibeah, the court of Saul, David was "a powerful man, a warrior, skilled in speech and handsome" (1 Sam 16:18). The combination of musician and warrior helps to explain not only his character but also his destiny.

David had many wives, the most famous being Bathsheba. In addition David had seven other wives named in the Bible including Michal, the daughter of Saul, as well as many other unnamed wives and concubines. His wives bore him many children: nineteen sons and one daughter named in the Bible, in addition to numerous unnamed sons and daughters (Howard: 41). No doubt David had a strong sexual appetite as recorded in the Bible.

David and Saul

The Bible does not accurately explain how David came to the attention of Saul. Was it his defeat of Goliath or his renown as a talented musician? First Samuel recounts the anointing of David by Samuel (16:1–13) and then his appearance in the royal court, implying a spiritual transfer of power from Saul to David. Whatever the basis, David soon became a confidant of Saul and his son Jonathan, even winning the hand of Michal, the daughter of Saul, in marriage. But when the exploits of David eclipsed that of Saul, the king could not endure the presence of David and tried to kill him (1 Sam 19:9–17). David had no choice but to flee and become an outlaw to Saul. Jonathan, however, the son of Saul, remained faithful to David (1 Sam 23:15–18) and David remained faithful to Jonathan and grieved over the death of his friend. David also grieved over the death of Saul (2 Sam 1:27), the one who tried to kill him. David easily expressed his emotions.

The Warrior

Since he had no family to return to in Bethlehem for support, David went where no one had authority, the fringes of civilization. He went into the wilderness and gathered some other misfits to create a band of soldiers. When living outside of the court, David became a mercenary, selling himself and his army to the northern tribes and taking their money, and assisting the southern tribes financially. David and his army lived on the booty and payment from military expeditions. He created for himself a type of leadership that eventually supported a strong kingship that he took for himself (Miller: 173). David's distribution of goods added to his power base and the more he gave away the stronger he became as a leader (Flanagan: 50). His authority lay in his ability to inspire other men like himself and instill an acceptance in lesser men. This may explain how he became king of Judah when anointed by the men of Judah in Hebron (2 Sam 2:1–4) and where he reigned for seven and a half years.

During the years of warfare with Saul, David had the opportunity to kill Saul but did not (1 Sam 24:2–23; 26:1–25). Being faithful to God, he could not bring himself to slay the anointed of God. Saul and Jonathan eventually die while fighting the Philistines. Jonathan is killed in battle and Saul falls on his sword rather than fall into the hands of his enemies (1 Sam 31). With the death of Saul, David seems to have in mind the unification of the two kingdoms under his one rule. After he had been anointed king in Hebron, he entered into negotiations with the lords of Jabeshgilead to show them he was interested in their allegiance (2 Sam 2:4b–7). But Abner, the commander of Saul's army, and Ishbaal, the son of Saul, jockeyed for power and suddenly they were assassinated. Did David arrange their deaths? (McCarter, 1986: 124–25). Surely he benefited the most from their demise, but no one can be sure he arranged to kill them. If so, he ascended to the throne through murder. Of course, David is not beyond murder as evident in the case of Uriah (2 Sam 11:1–27).

At this point representatives of Israel come to David at Hebron and he becomes the anointed king of all of Israel by the elders of the people, as recorded in 2 Samuel 5:1–5. David was thirty-three when he was anointed king of Israel. He reigned for forty years: first for seven and one-half years at Hebron and then for thirty-three years over Israel and Judah.

David and Jerusalem

Most people associate both Saul and David with Jerusalem. It seems true, however, that during the period of Saul, Jerusalem was a Jebusite city (2 Sam 5:6). David later captured it. The consummate politician wanted to rule over all of the tribes and needed a federal city to avoid tribal jealousy. He captured a neutral city and made it his capital. That way no one tribe could lay claim for special position in the newly established united kingdom. Situated between Israel and Judah, Jerusalem made a perfect geographical capital.

David enjoyed material success in Jerusalem favored both by God and the people (2 Sam 5:11–25). He enjoyed continued military success and he consolidated the territory both north and south. All of Second Samuel narrates the reign of David. Chapters 1–9 demonstrate how he consolidated his power and established an empire, with the second part of the book recording his many failures and how his own sons eventually weakened the kingdom (Boadt: 230–34).

David and the Ark

Jerusalem, established as the political capital, also needed to become the spiritual capital for the new kingdom. David brings the Ark of the Covenant to Jerusalem (2 Sam 6:1—7:29). During the journey David does his famous naked dance (2 Sam 6:14–23). The passage in question does not specify what David was wearing or not wearing. Was it a priestly garment, or a loincloth, or nothing? No certainty can be gained through the text but the context implies that David danced naked, especially because of the reaction of his wife Michal (2 Sam 6:20). When Uzzah touched the ark to support it and God struck him dead, David was afraid of God and left the ark at the house of Obededom. When he learned that God had blessed the house of Obededom, David determined to bring the ark to Jerusalem. Being fearful of the power of God may well have encouraged David to remove any sign of royalty in the presence of the ark. This would explain his dancing. The proud David suddenly, because of fear, becomes the humble David. Later generations would not have approved of such activity and thus we have the lack of clarity about what David wore. Dancing naked enthusiastically in the presence of the Ark of the Covenant would fit the personality of David nicely.

With the ark in Jerusalem and the cultic activity of the Zadokite priests under the control of David, he had accomplished his consolidation both politically and religiously. Only in Jerusalem would sacrifices be offered to God with the priests from the local high places coming into Jerusalem regularly to participate in the sacrifices, joined to the priests of David (Bright: 206). The ever-clever diplomat accomplished what he wanted and pleased people at the same time. No wonder David succeeded.

The Decline

The rest of the stories of David narrate his decline caused either by his own neglect or his personal sins, or finally, by his own sons. He continued to battle against the Ammonites, the Arameans, and the Syrians, finally reaching a peaceful settlement with all of them (2 Sam 10:18). Eventually he would have to battle against his son Absalom in a civil war. The turning point in the life of David, however, both politically and spiritually, resulted from his affair with Bathsheba.

David and Bathsheba

The Bible does not explain why David stayed home from his battles with the Ammonites. His presence in Jerusalem, however, afforded him the opportunity to see Bathsheba bathing and to not only desire her sexually but also actually to conceive a child with her (2 Sam 11:2–27). Desire and opportunity for sexual activity exist in most people's lives. In the lives of leaders the temptation may be greater but, provided desire and opportunity do not coincide, no great damage ensues. For David the desire and opportunity coincided when Uriah the husband of Bathsheba was out fighting for David. To cover his sin, David tried unsuccessfully to have Uriah sleep with his wife. Uriah would not engage in such activity while David's men were in battle. Finally David arranged for the death of Uriah by having his general Joab place Uriah in the heat of the battle lines, which caused his death. How much Bathsheba contributed to the opportunity remains unknown. In all probability, both had the desire and both sought out the opportunity. Both ultimately suffered, for the boy Bathsheba carried died shortly after birth (2 Sam 12:13–23; McCarter, 1980: 177).

God sent Nathan the prophet who by a clever parable brought David to admit what he had done because of his lust, and to do penance (2 Sam 12:1–7). David hoped that God would relent and spare the child. When God did not, David went to the house of the Lord and worshipped and then returned to his duties (2 Sam 12:23). The pious king fulfilled his obligations to God even if God did not answer his prayer. The oracle of Nathan predicting that evil would come to David from his own house (2 Sam 12:10–12) was fulfilled in the rebellion against David by his son Absalom. In this same chapter, however, God's grace returns to David in the birth of his son named Solomon, meaning peaceable, and Jedidiah, meaning beloved of God. (2 Sam 12:24–25). Peace and the beloved of God would be eternally joined to the house of David.

Rebellion

The further decline of David continues with the rebellion of his two sons Amnon and Absalom (2 Sam 13–19). Amnon rapes his half-sister Tamar and Absalom retaliates by killing Amnon and then flees to the town of his mother. From then on David did little to influence events. He mourned the loss of his two sons and ultimately had to flee his city because Absalom had begun an active campaign of subversion against his father. The confrontation between father and son took place in the forest of Ephraim in Gilead. No match for the seasoned troops of David, Joab defeated the dissidents and killed Absalom. The story ends with the poignant lament of the father over the death of the son:

> And the king was deeply moved, and went up to the chamber over the gate, and wept; and as he wept, he said, "O my son Absalom, my son, my son Absalom! Would I had died instead of you, O Absalom, my son, my son!" (2 Sam 18:33)

David's restoration as king brought only a limited success. There was further rebellion over succession by two other sons, Adonijah and Solomon. Eventually David favored Solomon. Adonijah, who had proclaimed kingship for himself, was deposed. Not content with his family problems, even in his old age David continued to anger God by attempting a census (2 Sam 14:1–25). David's pride once again caused problems (Knoppers: 449–70). God intended to punish David but allowed David to decide the punishment. At first, David chose to allow his people to suffer rather than he personally should suffer at the hands of his enemies. He finally saw what he had caused and asked God to punish him. David then purchased land, which would eventually become the place of the Temple of Solomon, and offered sacrifices. This averted the wrath of God and God lifted the plague. The pious David had returned to the scene.

The Death of David

David seems to finally have controlled his sexual appetite in his old age. When offered a virgin to keep him warm (1 Kgs 1:1–4) David "knew her not" (v. 4). The man who had more wives and concubines than were numbered, finally saw no need for further sexual activity. David was buried in his own city after having reigned as king for forty years.

> Then David slept with his fathers, and was buried in the city of David. And the time that David reigned over Israel was forty years; he reigned seven years in Hebron, and thirty-three years in Jerusalem. So Solomon sat on the throne of David his father; and his kingdom was firmly established. (1 Kgs 2:10–12)

The Historical David

The David of Chronicles is the idealized David of later generations. Even Samuel and Kings have been sifted over and expanded in the process of editing and compilation. No doubt his exploits and adventures were recorded to consolidate allegiance and add to his position in history. Most, however, believe that the books of Samuel and Kings contain much historical material about David and Solomon that truly express some of the events, even if exaggerated by history and retelling. While trying to be historical and accurate, contemporary readers should not accept motivations imposed by the narrator on some of the characters. No doubt David's motivation, like all people's, eludes easy explanation. Perhaps the career of a young man rising to considerable power can best be seen as a typical success story of the early Iron Age, similar to American stories of poor boys rising to success in the mold of

Horatio Alger. Some historical truth as a kernel, and perhaps many overlays, explain the true David.

Conclusion: The Poet/Warrior

David probably was a poet/warrior, full of ambition, using his talents to beguile followers. He united Israel and Judah under one king and he built an empire. He fought both in international campaigns with the decline of Egypt and fought a civil war with his sons. The international campaigns angered many neighboring kings and for Absalom to succeed even partially meant some were dissatisfied with David's rule. Maybe the poet/warrior could not manage the day-to-day affairs of state once he had brought everything together. Absalom warns the Israelites that they would get no hearing from the king (2 Sam 15:3) while Absalom claimed that he would be a sympathetic and responsive judge (vv. 3–4). David held on to his loyal supporters, probably joined to him by his earlier exploits and the power of the poet's personality. With them he reigned to the end.

He seems not to have thought too much about moral dilemmas. He lied, used people for his personal gain, and acted treacherously. His pride and ambition drove him to take what he wanted. He loved women, and Jonathan more than any woman (1 Sam 18:1–3; 2 Sam 1:26). Anger came to him easily and he even retreated from leading his men into battle, sending others to wage war for him.

Often indecisive in kingly affairs, he did not hesitate in personal affairs. He enjoyed both a life of leisure and a life of power. He was a repentant sinner at times and a pious king. He was an inspired prophet, a poet, and a warrior. He was a second Moses and First Solomon, a brilliant politician, and a morally frail person who sometimes had sincere remorse.

Above all, David was driven. He had a religious personality. He lived and died an honest sinner with a fierce love of life. Throughout his life he struggled with a mystical relationship to

God, that had to be suspended while he took on life in all its forms. At the end he succumbed to his relationship to God. He acknowledged how much he needed God and counseled Solomon to pay attention to God in how he lived:

> I am about to go the way of all the earth. Be strong, and show yourself a man, and keep the charge of the LORD your God, walking in his ways and keeping his statutes, his commandments, his ordinances, and his testimonies, as it is written in the law of Moses, that you may prosper in all that you do and wherever you turn; that the LORD may establish his word which he spoke concerning me, saying, "If your sons take heed to their way, to walk before me in faithfulness with all their heart and with all their soul, there shall not fail you a man on the throne of Israel." (1 Kgs 2:2–4)

David had many flaws and many noble traits, and of all the men and women in the Old Testament, God loved David above them all.

Topics for Discussion

1. Do you know any poet/warriors? What do you think of such people? Are you one?

2. Why would some people want to cover up the weaknesses of David? Does this still happen today?

3. David never saw a sin he did not like. Good or bad?

4. Did David repent permanently, or did he continue to repent? How does that affect you?

5. The poet wins but only at the end of his life. Why is that tragic?

6. David seems to have enjoyed sex a great deal. How does this fit his personality?

7. Do you like David or not? Give your reasons to be for or against the one that God loved above all.

Works Consulted

Boadt, Lawrence. *Reading the Old Testament: An Introduction.* New York/Mahwah, NJ: Paulist Press, 1984.

Bright, John. *A History of Israel.* Philadelphia: Westminster Press, 1981.

Brueggemann, Walter. *First and Second Samuel.* Louisville, KY: John Knox Press, 1990.

Flanagan, J. W. "Succession and Genealogy in the Davidic Dynasty." In *The Quest of the Kingdom of God,* edited by H. B. Huffmon. Winona Lakes, IN: Eisenbrauns, 1982, 35–55.

Howard, David M. "David," *The Anchor Bible Dictionary,* vol. 2. New York: Doubleday, 1992, 41–49.

Knoppers, Gary. "Images of David in Early Judaism: David as Repentant Sinner in Chronicles." *Biblica* 76 (1995): 449–70.

McCarter, P. Kyle. "The Historical David." *Interpretation* 40 (1986): 117–29.

———. *2 Samuel.* New York: Doubleday, 1980.

Miller, J. M. "Saul's rise to power: Some observations concerning 1 Sam 9:1–10:16; 10:26–11:15 and 13:2–14:46." *Catholic Biblical Quarterly* 36 (1974): 157–74.

Chapter Five

Isaiah

Many people recognize words and phrases from Isaiah. Anyone who has listened to Handel's *Messiah* knows many verses from Isaiah:

> For unto us a child is born, unto us a son is given....
> And his name shall be called, "Wonderful Counselor....
> Everlasting Father, Prince of Peace."

Anyone who has paid attention to many of the readings during the season of Advent will find many parts of Isaiah familiar. Even artists, such as Brueghel in his *Peaceable Kingdom,* have painted the vision of Isaiah. Then:

> The wolf shall dwell with the lamb,
>   and the leopard shall lie down with the kid,
> and the calf and the lion and the fatling together,
>   and a little child shall lead them. (Isa 11:6)

The book of Isaiah is the longest in the Old Testament and was probably finally put together during the third century before Christ. Many have divided the book into three sections and three periods. The earliest chapters (1–39) come from the time of political unrest in the eighth century before Christ. The middle section comes from chapters 40–55, from the mid-sixth century and the exile in Babylon, and the final section (56–66) from the last quarter of the sixth century before Christ (Seitz: 472). Throughout the whole period political crises proliferate. Great nations come and go in shame, but God's power and reign remain solid and eternal. A remnant of Israel will always remain faithful. God will redeem them, not for their own sake but because of the fidelity of God bringing about a manifestation of God's power and goodness. People see the glory of God:

> And the glory of the LORD shall be revealed,
>   and all flesh shall see it together,
>   for the mouth of the LORD has spoken. (Isa 40:5)

The book offers little biographical information about its author. Isaiah experienced the presence of God in the Temple sometime around 742 BC (Isa 6). At times he engaged in bizarre actions such as walking naked and barefooted (Isa 20:1ff.). Perhaps he had a number of followers (Isa 8:16) but this need not be so. Isaiah probably came from Jerusalem and went to a school for scribes (Isa 30:8). He also probably came from a powerful family because of his ease with dealing with the king, and he might have been related to the king. If he was part of the court, most of his life he stood in opposition to the king and his policies and rebuked the king in the harshest terms. Isaiah married and had children to whom he gave symbolic names: Isaiah 7:3: *she'ar yashuv* (a remnant shall return); Isaiah 7:14: *Immanuel* (God is with us [some think Emmanuel was not the child of Isaiah: Seitz, 1993: 60–75]); and Isaiah 8:3: and *maher shalal hash baz* (speed, spoil, plunder). Most of his personal life hides in shadows. The book manifests little concerning relationships with wife and children, but also offers no evidence of loneliness or sadness. Rather the opposite seems true. Isaiah, perhaps more than anyone else in the Bible, lives with an unbridled optimism. For fifty years Isaiah towered over his contemporaries and more than any other person of the time, gave guidance to his country through a dark and perilous period. The reading of the book of Isaiah offers insights into his personality.

The Unity of the Book of Isaiah

Although most scholars accept the book as written by different individuals over a two-hundred-year period (Clifford, 1993: 2–17), the book has its own unity. A sense of optimism characterizes the entire book. The prophet can sit on a pile of rubble and believe it will all be rebuilt. He can look at a barren desert and proclaim that the desert will be in bloom. He can recognize the sins of the people and preach the goodness of God and a future which will be better (Boadt: 327–31). Throughout the entire book the various authors always find reason for hope. Even in the presence of dire situations caused by human failures, the entire book of Isaiah offers comfort and consolation. Even the servant songs in Second Isaiah with their inevitable suffering can never take away from the overriding optimism. Suffering can be positive, for through suffering much good can come.

The Religious Experience of Isaiah

Chapter 6 narrates Isaiah's experience of God (Knierem: 47–68). Uzziah the king had died and the political scene was filled with anxiety, fear, and clouds of coming doom. The prophet is in the Temple and he experiences the holiness of God. The vision seems physical, spiritual, and intellectual. The scene contains all of the elements of a theophany: fire, smoke, light, clouds, ministering members of the divine court, and a radical change in the person.

William James, as already noted, recognizes four elements as part of the mystical or religious experience: the moment cannot be named, the person learns something about self and God, the person is passive, and it all passes quickly. Rudolf Otto speaks of the *mysterium tremens,* in which the person becomes frightened, and *mysterium fascinans,* in which the person remains transfixed and fascinated. Isaiah experienced all of the above.

...I saw the LORD sitting upon a throne, high and lifted up;...Above him stood the seraphim; each had six wings.... (Isa 6:1–2)

The seraphim were mythological creatures associated with foreign gods, probably from Assyria. They had wings and a body which combined human and animal elements. During this period perhaps the syncretism of the temple worship permitted these creatures to be displayed as statues in the temple area, and now these ministers of the foreign gods serve the one true God. The Septuagint (Greek translation of the Old Testament) has the seraphim around the throne and not above the throne of God. The God of Israel controls all other gods and all of those who minister to those gods.

The seraphim have six wings. Two wings veil their face in the presence of God, two others veil the genitals in God's presence, and with two they fly. They call out the transcendence of God with the triple *Kadosh:* holy, holy, holy. *Kadosh* (which is translated as holy) in root means to be cut off or separated. God is cut off or separated from all that is not God. The triple repetition of *holy* signifies the intensity of God's otherness in comparison to Isaiah. The seraphim also acknowledge that God is the God of armies (hosts) and the fullness of the earth is filled with God's power and goodness (glory). Finally they purify Isaiah for his mission. The prophet acknowledges his uncleanness in the midst of unclean people and after he has been purified by fire, he willingly accepts his divine mission (Heschel: 89–90).

The Mission of Isaiah

Isaiah begins by denouncing the lack of fidelity to the Law of the Lord. He foresees only doom coming to Judah if they continue on their present path. The prophet seems almost overwhelmed with the national sin. With fury he denounced the powerful nobles and the venal judges who conspired to rob the unfortunate of their rights and dignity (Isa 1:21–23; 3:13–15; 5:8; 10:1–4). The king in particular trusts more in historical maneuvering than in God. The king wants to play with the powerful nations of north and south and ultimately becomes a vassal of Assyria. Instead of trusting in God, he trusts in himself;

> Is it too little for you to weary men, that you must also weary my God? (Isa 7:13)

The more Isaiah preaches, the more people refuse to believe, and yet he never loses his sense of optimism. At times he must have experienced frustration, but his sense of God as the ultimate future never leaves him. His third son, whom he calls *spoils* and *plunder*, has to be seen in relationship to the names of his other sons: *the remnant shall return* and *God is with us*. He knows the devastation will be total, and yet:

> The wilderness and the dry land shall be glad,
>   the desert shall rejoice and blossom;
> like the crocus it shall blossom abundantly,
>   and rejoice with joy and singing.
> The glory of Lebanon shall be given to it,
>   the majesty of Carmel and Sharon.
> They shall see the glory of the LORD,
>   the majesty of our God. (Isa 35:1–2)

Remember the period: violent war, political and religious corruption, infidelity to God, and persecution of the poor and lonely together with those who try to remain faithful. The entire book is filled with oracles of doom and gloom, which people bring upon themselves. The prophet knew that politics can never solve the problem of a lack of justice. Politics itself, with its arrogance and its lack of concern for the oppressed, was the problem. Politics functions on the power of the sword. Political alliances involve preparations for war and that means brutalities and carnage. War spawns death and not life. Yet, Isaiah never loses sight of the power and goodness of God. The prophet remains both faithful and hopeful. God is the ultimate future of the human race and no sin by any number of people can ever destroy what God has already planned for creation and for the human race. God alone offers true protection.

Isaiah and the Future: Peace and the Just Ruler

The ancient Greek proverb notes that the sign of a great civilization is when people plant trees under whose shade they will never sit. The prophet Isaiah lived that proverb. He planted the trees of faith and hope in the midst of human infidelity and corruption. He foresaw a time when not only would the animals live in peace, but all people would live in peace:

> He shall judge between the nations,
>   and shall decide from many peoples;
> and they shall beat their swords into plowshares,
>   and their spears into pruning hooks,
> nation shall not lift up sword against nation,
>   neither shall they learn war any more. (Isa 2:4)

Isaiah had his religious experience of God and accepted his divine mandate to preach against sin and corruption. His words for the most part fell on deaf ears. People did not want to change. Political and religious leaders were content with what they had and jealous of losing anything they possessed. They sought security in political alliances rather than trust in God, and they suffered the consequences.

Frequently Isaiah took on the high and mighty and frequently he encountered rejection. He could have become angry and frustrated with God. He could have held on to little hope for the future. Instead, he remained faithful to what he believed. He trusted in God and never once wavered in his commitment to a better future, however faraway that future might be.

People live in hope for a righteous and just leader to bring about peace and prosperity. In the Old Testament and in the

Middle Ages, every time a new king began to rule, people hoped that this one would finally be the right one who could bring justice and peace to all people. Each time, often after only a brief period, the people would recognize that this king was not the right one. They would have to wait for another.

The same is true for all times. No religious leader, no political leader, no business leader is the one who will bring perfect justice, peace, and prosperity to all. God alone will send the one just ruler who will provide security and stability, justice and truth. Throughout Isaiah God speaks of this coming One who will fulfill all of human hopes for a good future.

> For to us a child is born,
>   to us a son is given;
> and the government shall be upon his shoulder,
>   and his name will be called
> "Wonderful Counselor, Mighty God,
>   Everlasting Father, Prince of Peace."
> Of the increase of his government and of peace
>   there will be no end,
> upon the throne of David, and over his kingdom,
>   to establish it, and to uphold it
> with justice and righteousness
>   from this time forth and for evermore.
> The zeal of the LORD of hosts will do this. (Isa 9:6–7)

The Servant Songs

One additional element in the words of Isaiah and the future has to be added. Although not written by the same person as the first thirty-nine chapters, the four Servant songs (Clifford, 1992: 499–500) in the second part of Isaiah (Isa 42:1–9; 49:1–6; 50:4–9; 52:13—53:12) add the element of suffering to the one who not only believes in the good future but also works to accomplish it. The period is the Babylonian exile and the author joins earlier Isaiah in his sense of optimism. He knows God has a glorious plan for good in the future but also knows that anyone who strives to accomplish the vision of Isaiah will endure suffering. No one who contributes to the good of others can do so without personal investment and often with much personal suffering. The true follower of God, like the candle, will be consumed in the effort to give light to others. The Servant in Isaiah fulfilled this destiny. Christians automatically related the Servant of God to Jesus. Others see the Servant as not just one historical person, but anyone who acknowledges dependence on God and who works for the salvation of others. Both are true. Jesus epitomizes what others have done in the past and in the present and will continue to do in the future. To bring God's saving presence to others will always involve personal suffering.

The Fidelity of God

Isaiah loved God. He loved Jerusalem and the whole country of Israel. He believed in the restoration of all things, even in the midst of human wantonness and destruction. He knew moral corruption from within would destroy everything without. But God could never abandon Sion, Jerusalem, or the people. Isaiah's trust of God remained ever strong and so he could never believe that the nation's sins could frustrate the divine plan and annul the promises of old. Suffering will always precede purification and faith brings a sense of calm. A remnant, a small group, will always remain faithful for they continue to believe that God is with them.

Isaiah the Man

To live in a world of pain and suffering and not give in to despair costs much. Hope should not disappoint but often does. Isaiah witnessed the failure of leaders both religious and civil. He watched as the wealthy used their power to gain more wealth and oppress the poor. He experienced war and lived through destruction. The hope of Isaiah rested on his experience of God. Isaiah was a religious man who worshipped in the Temple. God rewarded him with a religious experience which gave him the support to fulfill his ministry in the presence of opposition and suffering. Frequently denied the companionship of loving family and friends, he never lost sight of "what might be," even if it never was. Certainly no one person wrote the whole book of Isaiah, and it might be unfair to try to assemble one personality from the various sections of this book, but the book does have its unity. Whoever put it together combined the understanding of God and the experience of peoples and created a unity. Maybe the Isaiah of the book is a phantom: a combination of the virtues of several people, or an ideal to which all people should strive to emulate. No one finds it easy to live with hope in a world teeming with corruption and destruction, but Isaiah the prophet did just that. To sit on a pile of rubble and proclaim "this will be rebuilt" ennobles the human spirit. "To dream the impossible dream, ...to bear with unbearable sorrow, to run where the brave dare not go" (words and music by Leigh/Darion) is usually associated with Don Quixote from the musical *Man of La Mancha*. The Spanish knight had a predecessor in Isaiah.

Conclusion

Sometime around 688 BCE Sennacherib invaded Judah a second time. Isaiah supported King Hezekiah and encouraged him to stand firm. The prophet believed strongly that Assyria had gone too far. The foreigners had exhausted the patience of God and had blasphemed God (Isa 37:21–29) and would not be allowed to take Jerusalem (Isa 29:5–8; 37:33–35). The king stood firm and Sennacherib did not take the city. Then the old prophet and author of the first section of Isaiah fades from view. A late tradition has Isaiah martyred by Manasseh, but no historical evidence can support this claim. Second and Third Isaiah eventually saw the destruction of Jerusalem and the complete failure of people to trust in their

God, and they ended up in exile in a foreign land. It was all over. But maybe not.

God will do something new and good. The arid desert will blossom into vibrant colors. The soft rain will nourish the hidden life living just beneath the surface. People will learn not war but peace. Their weapons of destruction will become utensils for peace. The future will begin in the present, even if the fullness of the future remains a distant goal. Suffering inevitably comes to those who live faithfully. But suffering brings purification and an awareness of the need for God. God's servants, like Isaiah, know that human life brings its problems, but God still beckons into a good future. Isaiah lived and died the servant of God who never lost his optimism and trust in the midst of human failure and sin. The lamb may not yet lie down with the lion, but it will!

Topics for Discussion

1. Is Isaiah really the eternal optimist?

2. What verses from Isaiah do you particularly like?

3. How can people remain positive in the midst of evil and sin?

4. Who was the Servant of God? Is it Jesus? Good people in general?

5. Do you think God is the future of the human race?

6. God remains faithful. Is this evident in history?

7. Did Isaiah predict a messiah in particular or in general? What were some of the characteristics of this messiah in Isaiah?

Works Consulted

Boadt, Lawrence. *Reading the Old Testament: An Introduction.* New York/Mahwah, NJ: Paulist Press, 1984.

Clifford, Richard. "Isaiah, Book of (Second Isaiah)," *The Anchor Bible Dictionary*. New York: Doubleday, 1992, 490–501.

———. "The Unity of the Book of Isaiah and Its Cosmogonic Language." *Catholic Biblical Quarterly* 55 (1993): 1–17.

Heschel, Abraham. *The Prophets*. Peabody, MA: Hendrickson, 2000.

Knierim, Rolf. "The Vocation of Isaiah." *Vetus Testamentum* 18 (1968): 47–68.

Seitz, Christopher. "Isaiah, Book of (First Isaiah)," *The Anchor Bible Dictionary*. New York: Doubleday, 1992, 472–88.

———. *Isaiah 1–39*. Louisville, KY: John Knox, 1993.

Chapter Six

Jeremiah

Jeremiah, the reluctant prophet, the prophet who suffered both from persecution and a divine imperative to speak and act, lived during the last period of Israel/Judah from approximately 640–597 BCE. He survived the destruction of Jerusalem in 587 and lived out the rest of his life as an exile in Egypt. "No braver or more tragic figure ever trod the stage of Israel's history than the prophet Jeremiah" (Bright: 333).

Jeremiah lived during a tumultuous period in the history of Israel and Judah. Previously, under Assyria, changes took place in the Ancient Near East and then Babylon became the dominant political power. During the brief period between the power struggle from Assyria to Babylon Israel inaugurated short-lived religious reform under King Josiah. The freedom and reform, however, was short lived. After Josiah's death, former repudiated religious practices returned and the actual demise of the kingdom came quickly in the destruction of the city of Jerusalem in 587.

Seduction and Rape

Perhaps no other verse in the book of Jeremiah, and possibly in the entire Old Testament, reflects so much frustration and even anger with God as does Jeremiah's lament in chapter 20:7:

O LORD, thou hast deceived me,
   and I was deceived;
thou art stronger than I,
   and thou hast prevailed.
I have become a laughingstock all the day;
   every one mocks me. (RSV)

You duped me, O LORD, and I let myself be duped;
   you were too strong for me, and you triumphed.
All the day I am an object of laughter;
   everyone mocks me. (NAB)

You have seduced me, Yahweh, and I have let myself be
   seduced;
you have overpowered me: you were the stronger.
I am a daily laughing-stock;
   everybody's butt. (Jerusalem)

Heschel (113) more honestly translated the verse:

O Lord, Thou hast seduced me and I am seduced.
Thou hast raped me and I am overcome.

Heschel accurately explains the relationship between God and
Jeremiah. It began with the sweetness of seduction and ended with
the violence of rape (Heschel: 114). Has anyone in the Bible
described the human/divine relationship in stronger terms? The
use of the Hebrew word *patah* acknowledges that the seduction
was by far not against the will, but implies that the prophet gave
his consent only after allurements and enticement. Jeremiah experienced both the enticement by God and then suffered the violence
of the violated. Jeremiah may well have screamed at God:
"Enough is enough. Leave me alone. All I have are problems and
pain." The angry, frustrated prophet rails against God only to turn
into his own heart and in anguish proclaim:

If I say I will not mention him
   or speak any more in his name

there is in my heart as it were a burning fire
    shut up in my bones
and I am weary with holding it in
    and I cannot. (Jer 20:9; RSV)

The reluctant prophet suffered from the divine imperative. He could *not* not fulfill his destiny as a conscience for Israel. And so Jeremiah suffered rejection, isolation, persecution, and dishonor. He also talked back to God and told God precisely how he felt. Jeremiah lived as the reluctant prophet, and also the prophet who epitomized what many people have felt in their relationship to God over the centuries.

The Life of the Prophet

The book of Jeremiah offers significant information on the life of the prophet (Bright: 334). Jeremiah's father was a priest possibly descended from Abithar, a priest of David. Since the family owned land (Jer 32:9) as well as being in the priestly line, Jeremiah's youth may well have been one of privilege. Called to be a prophet around 627 BCE, the young Jeremiah probably was around 12 or 13, similar to the call of Samuel in age. In fact, both prophets shared a common linkage to the high place at Shiloh. Similarities also between Jeremiah and Moses support the idea that the prophet saw himself as a "prophet like Moses." The vision before the almond tree (Jer 1:11–12) recalls Moses and the burning bush. Jeremiah's protestation that he cannot speak (Jer 1:6) reminds the reader of the same protest by Moses.

Jeremiah offers no sign of accepting his call as a prophet. In fact the call contrasts significantly with Isaiah. With Isaiah, God asks whom he shall send and Isaiah replies send me (Isa 6:8–9). Jeremiah seems to have no choice.

"Before I formed you in the womb I knew you,
and before you were born I consecrated you;
I appointed you a prophet to the nations." (Jer 1:5)

God made the decision and Jeremiah had to accept. God goes further and reminds Jeremiah: "I am watching over my word to perform it" (Jer 1:12). Only later, perhaps as long as five years, does Jeremiah accept and eat the scroll. At that time he accepted his call (Lundbom: 686–87).

> Your words were found, and I ate them, and your words became to me a joy and the delight of my heart.... (Jer 15:16)

From this period on Jeremiah preached in Jerusalem and remained there until the city fell in 587 BCE.

The precise relationship between Jeremiah and the official court, both religious and political, remains unclear (Lundbom: 687–88). At times he seems to have supported the official worship, and at other times has grave reservations. Often he appears isolated and lonely and certainly he suffered persecution. Chapter 1 uses strong verbs to describe what Jeremiah must do: pluck up and break down, destroy and overthrow (Jer 1:10b,c). The harshness is somewhat tempered by the final two verbs: build and plant (Jer 1:10d), but there was no doubt that Jeremiah would cause so much resentment that he would mostly have to suffer. Before any message of hope would come, destruction must come first.

Jeremiah and His Confessions

Throughout his career Jeremiah struggled with his relationship to God. His famous confessions display the full gamut of emotions from anger and resentment, hatred and sorrow, fear and despair, to love and joy, courage and hope (Boadt: 371–72). Chapter 11 first recounts the evil that people have brought upon themselves, and then the prophet acknowledges his own pain caused by others. They have plotted against Jeremiah; he was like a gentle lamb led to the slaughter (Jer 11:19a). They sought to remove him not only from life but also from history (Jer 11:19b). In his anger the prophet wants God to punish them for all they had done to him. The anger and resentment of the prophet heats up in the following chapter (Jer 12) with the question: Why does God allow the wicked to prosper? Jeremiah wants God to slaughter them. He is tired of speaking to people who will not listen and calls upon God to do something for the sake of the promise of old. God speaks (Jer 12:7–17), but Jeremiah is not content with the evil that comes to the wicked as a result of their own wickedness. Jeremiah wants immediate action from God to destroy the wicked. The pain they brought upon themselves does not suffice for Jeremiah. He wants more. But God does not oblige the prophet.

The Troubled Prophet

Jeremiah experiences ever-growing isolation (Jer 15:10–20). Crisis follows crisis and the deception of others characterizes the life of the prophet. He laments his birth for he has become a man of strife and contention to the whole land (Jer 15:10). He sits alone among merrymakers for God filled Jeremiah with indignation (Jer 15:17). Even God seems deceitful to him (Jer 15:18).

Discouraged by human failure, Jeremiah complains again to God (Jer 17:14–18). He needs healing and a refuge from those who persecute him. He wants others to suffer instead of him suffering; he desires God to shame the evildoers who persecute him, and destroy them. The call to pluck and break down, destroy and overthrow has overwhelmed the call to build and plant (Jer 1:10). Jeremiah's lament continues (18:18–23) with further persecution and a renewed call to God to destroy the evildoers who are persecuting him.

Jeremiah feels that God has betrayed him and so the people can have a field day with the "so-called" prophet. His own people laugh and scorn him; they refuse to listen to any of his prophecies announcing violence and destruction, and Jeremiah longs to be free from his responsibility and no longer to speak in the name of God, but he cannot (Jer 20:9). Threatened by pain and even death (Jer 38:15), the isolated prophet (Jer 15:17) knows he cannot marry (Jer 16:2), will be deprived of the presence of wife and children, will experience rejection (Jer 25:3), and finally will see the city of Jerusalem destroyed and then go into exile into Egypt.

Throughout the book Jeremiah seems like a gentle man whom God forces to be harsh. He does not believe in force in religion, but when people freely reject his words he becomes angry and wants God to destroy them. He witnessed his country move from subjugation to a breath of freedom to final subjugation and destruction. Anguish characterized his life and personality. Jeremiah became bitter against the clergy who settled for empty ritual. He preached doom and experienced it personally.

The words of Jeremiah express great poetry (Lundbom: 692–97, 709) with light and hope and tenderness and faith, and stubborn courage in the midst of doom. The prophet loses patience and becomes intolerant and embittered. Often frustrated and near to despair, he seems a heroic failure. He has had enough of God and lacks inner peace. Finally he recognizes that he can meet God only in his own heart.

Jeremiah and the Future

But like all the great prophets before him, Jeremiah looks to a better future. People failed, but God remains constant. The one God of Israel and Judah will restore the people. Chapters 31–35 offer a final hope for all, including the reluctant prophet. Doom, sin, and judgment form the bulk of the message of Jeremiah. But throughout this dark message lies the presence of hope and salvation, and the presence of a loving and forgiving God (Lundbom: 719–21). In the beginning God had promised salvation (Jer 1:8) and repeated this pledge (Jer 1:19; 15:20–21). Jeremiah prayed for God's saving presence to the nation and gave thanks to God for offering hope (Jer 17:14–18; 20:11–13). The earliest preaching by Jeremiah recalled God's previous grace to Israel (Jer 2:6–7). Even when the Babylonians destroyed the city of Jerusalem, salvation became a hope for the exiles (Jer 30:5—31:22).

God will again restore the people of Israel (Clements: 184–93). They will be God's people and find grace in the wilderness (Jer 31:1–2). God's love remains everlasting (Jer 31:3). Jeremiah buys a field for the future (Jer 32:6–15) and God declares:

"Behold, the days are coming, says the LORD, when I will make a new covenant with the house of Israel and the house of Judah, not like the covenant which I made with their fathers when I took them by the hand to bring them out of the land of Egypt, my covenant which they broke, though I was their husband, says the LORD. But this is the covenant which I will make with the house of Israel after those days, says the LORD. I will put my law within them, and I will write it upon their hearts; and I will be their God and they shall be my people. And no longer shall each man teach his neighbor and each his brother, saying, 'Know the LORD,' for they shall all know me, from the least of them to the greatest, says the LORD; for I will forgive their iniquity, and I will remember their sin no more." (Jer 31:31–34)

Behold, I will gather them from all the countries to which I drove them in my anger and my wrath and in great indignation; I will bring them back to this place, and I will make them dwell in safety. And they shall be my people, and I will be their God. I will give them one heart and one way, that they may fear me for ever, for their own good and the good of their children after them. I will make with them an everlasting covenant, that I will not turn away from doing well to them; and I will put the fear of me in their hearts, that they may not turn from me. I will rejoice in doing them good, and I will plant them in the land in faithfulness, with all my heart and all my soul. (Jer 32:37–41)

> In those days and at that time I will cause a righteous
> Branch to spring forth for David; and he shall execute
> justice and righteousness in the land. In those days
> Judah will be saved and Jerusalem will dwell securely.
> (Jer 33:15–16a)

All will know God. God will write instruction in their hearts
and the following of the law of God will flow spontaneously from
within. The relationship between God and the people of Israel will
become like husband and wife and between parents and first-born.
All the sins will be forgiven and forgotten, for God will embrace
the people as wayward children and restore their well-being. God
will rejoice in doing good for the people, and a final and everlasting love and communion will characterize God and the holy
people of Israel and Judah. The building and planting will take
place, but only after the people have fallen to their knees in need.
Doom will come but will not last. God has spoken and God will
not allow the word to be frustrated.

Jeremiah's Personality

Jeremiah had a religious personality. His very being cried out
for a profound and deeply personal relationship to God and God
responded. Psychologically, Jeremiah could not always assimilate
this relationship, especially as he attempted to fulfill his ministry
to a people who not only ignored him but also persecuted him.
A driven person, Jeremiah could not abide the stupidity of his
countrymen and often withdrew into himself and suffered from
loneliness and depression.

Like Isaiah, Jeremiah developed a close relationship with
God. But unlike Isaiah, God seems to have given Jeremiah no
choice. Isaiah experienced God in the Temple and the prophet vol-
unteered to speak in the name of God. Poor Jeremiah was destined
to do so from his mother's womb (Jer 1:5). Whether he liked it or
not, he seems to have had no choice. Even running away from God

could not last. Also like Isaiah, Jeremiah witnessed the corruption of religious and civil leaders, the oppression of the poor, and the terrible effects of war. Often his hope seemed to evaporate, only to return after the prophet had suffered some more. Deprived of family and friends Jeremiah lived a lonely and painful life, desiring only the simplest pleasures and often finding nothing.

Jeremiah hoped his relationship with God would always support him in his problems, but then he felt that even God had abandoned him to pain and suffering. He rejoiced in a relationship with God that brought sweetness and enticement, joy and pleasure, only to experience the violence of being ripped apart both spiritually and psychologically by this same God. Frustrated, impatient, angry, and highly emotional, Jeremiah longed for a peaceful restoration of all that was good and holy, and ended his life in exile in Egypt. He lived and died in the midst of human failure and personal defeat, but still had hope (Clements: 3; Boadt: 373–74). Eventually he acknowledged that God would be the final cause of joy and people would benefit not by anything they did or did not do, but only because of what God had decided to do. Jeremiah held on to a future hope of justice and righteousness, fidelity and peace, that God alone would accomplish. The reluctant prophet lived the divine imperative with a great mixture of hope and despair, love and hatred, joy and sorrow, fear and boldness, with his anger and frustration finally giving way to a peaceful acceptance of the presence of God in his life. In spite of all of Jeremiah's problems, he remains a good model for anyone who allows God to be a presence in human life.

Topics for Discussion

1. Is it difficult to be a prophet?

2. Does God treat Jeremiah fairly?

3. Can seduction and rape characterize a relationship with God?

4. Have you ever experienced a divine imperative?

5. Should people talk to God as Jeremiah did?

6. Why was Jeremiah so angry?

7. How should one combine anger with hope?

8. What appeals to you as you read Jeremiah? What causes trouble for you?

Works Consulted

Boadt, Lawrence. *Reading the Old Testament: An Introduction*. New York/Mahwah, NJ: Paulist Press, 1984.

Bright, John. *A History of Israel*. Philadelphia: Westminster Press, 1981.

Clements, R. E. *Jeremiah*. Atlanta: John Knox, 1988.

Heschel, Abraham. *The Prophets*. Peabody, MA: Hendrickson, 2000.

Lundbom, Jack R. "Jeremiah," *The Anchor Bible Dictionary*. New York: Doubleday, 1992.

PART III

Men in the
New Testament

The stories of men in the New Testament differ significantly from those in the Old Testament. First, the period extends for less than a hundred years. Actually most of the stories told are from a period of less than forty years, from approximately 29 CE to 62 CE. The characters taken together help explain the origins of Christianity as a religion in a relatively brief period. They all come from the same Jewish religious tradition and the same limited geography. Like the stories in the Old Testament, however, they also come from documents written from the perspective of the religion, and like the Old Testament, the individuals and their stories often had additions or omissions that catered to what the writers wanted to say to their audiences. Even in the New Testament, sometimes hyperbole adds further dimensions to simple stories.

A study of men in the New Testament must include Jesus of Nazareth. No other man in the Bible has had more influence in human history than Jesus. He divided history into the period before him (BC, before Christ), and the period after him (AD, year of the Lord). Even the more recent use of Common Era (CE) and Before the Common Era (BCE) fails to disguise the chronological division based on Jesus of Nazareth. But who is Jesus? A careful reading of the four gospels shows different portraits or images of Jesus. Each gospel has its own way of telling the reader something about Jesus.

Over the past two centuries individuals have struggled with the search for the historical Jesus. Who was he? How did he live? What can anyone know about his personality? Every student of Christianity knows that Christians have experienced for the past two thousand years not the Jesus of Nazareth but the Christ of Christian faith, that is, how people of faith expressed their understanding of Jesus based on their commitment to him more than on the actual historical person. These students know that the New Testament can never be accepted as a historical biographical document but rather, the New Testament persists in its claim to offer assistance to a troubled world as a faith document. Yet, in reading the gospels people can come to some appreciation of the life, ministry, and personality of Jesus.

The Historical Jesus

The studies of the nineteenth century that sought first to discover an actual biography of Jesus, and then a psychology of Jesus, were doomed. The earthly Jesus is the one who actually lived in ancient Israel. This involves his family, friends, daily life, actual preaching, and death—and the reaction of his friends after his death. The historical Jesus or the Jesus of history is the earthly life of Jesus as reconstructed historiographically through the means of modern historical critical scholarship. The Christ of faith is the risen, empowered Son of God, giver of the Spirit, and founder of the Christian Church proclaimed in the church. Each differs considerably from the other. Yet each depends on the other.

The recent studies by Meier and Crossan have opened once again the quest for the historical Jesus. More information from the discovery of ancient documents, especially at Nag Hammadi; more studies on the social environment of the first century; greater knowledge of linguistics and the various uses of language have all contributed to the rethinking of the historical Jesus, as well as the earthly Jesus. But who was the real Jesus?

Contemporary Christians may find it difficult to accept how limited the knowledge of Jesus, the source of Christianity, actually is. At the foundation level, historians can only state that Jesus lived in Palestine, was known as a good man, and was crucified (Kee: chapter 1). Many of the ideas Christians associate with Jesus: virginal conception, bodily resurrection, healing and raising from the dead, his preaching and his relationship to God, come more from his followers than Jesus historically, and eventually these beliefs gave to future generations the New Testament. Yet, reading the gospels does give us insights into who he was and how he understood himself.

God as Abba

Joachim Jeremias has devoted much of his life to the study of the religious experience of Jesus. For Jeremias, Jesus used *Abba* regularly as his personal form of address for God (Jeremias: 61–67). Schillebeeckx speaks of the "abba principle" as the foundation of the self-understanding of Jesus and his mission (256–69). More recently Bernard Cooke writes of Jesus' abba experience (1–24). The conclusion generally accepted by both New Testament scholars and theologians alike recognizes that the self-understanding of Jesus rests upon an awareness of his special relationship to God. God loved him in a way unlike other people. Jesus was God's beloved. Jesus was the human face of God (O'Grady, 1994: 175–96). Such an awareness does not in any way imply that Jesus saw himself as equal to God, but rather that God had entered into his life in a most unusual way. Neither the self-awareness of Jesus nor the New Testament teaches that Jesus was the Second Person of the Blessed Trinity. This teaching developed after the apostolic period. Rather, in the New Testament, Jesus had a unique relationship to God characterized by his use of the word *abba* when he addressed God. Later reflection on this distinctive way of relating to God assisted the New Testament writers in presenting Jesus as the Son of God, Messiah, and Lord of all.

Images of Jesus in the New Testament

Some have seen Jesus as a political revolutionary, dedicated to the overthrow of the Roman authority in Israel. Recent studies have attempted to recover the Jewishness of Jesus, seeing him as a Jewish charismatic, or as a monastic Essene, or a rabbi, or even a proto-Pharisee, or as a Jew in the tradition of Old Testament prophets. The New Testament gives evidence, more or less, for all of these approaches except the political revolutionary. To them can be added the more traditional images as the kind and passionate savior, or the suffering human being, the teacher, the benevolent shepherd, the friend of outcasts. The New Testament also has many titles for Jesus: Messiah, Christ, Lord, Son of God, Son of Man, Son. And so the list goes on. The New Testament comes from the pens of many authors over at least a seventy-year time period. During this period development took place as the early followers of Jesus realized more and more the meaning that his life and message had for themselves and for future generations (Brown).

Jesus and His Followers

Even those who were privileged to know Jesus and to live with him and learn from him were limited in their appreciation of him. The New Testament authors do not display harmony in their sayings about Jesus. These documents come from a specific time and place. They are human documents, with all the defects and limitations of any human accomplishment. The careful reader can certainly gain much from a study of the New Testament in a search for Jesus, but that includes an awareness of the historical ambit, the social and cultural and religious milieu of Jesus' time and place.

God chose to act with people in a human way. Thus, the gospels would have to be limited and expressed within certain spiritual ideas common to all people. The Word was made flesh, but not flesh in general. Jesus was a man, a Jew born in a specific era in a particular country. What he did and what he taught have been expressed in human terms, taken from that time and that region, and thus part of the heritage of Judaism.

The first preachers of Jesus also lived within the confines of a particular education and culture. When Jesus spoke of God he did so in terms of his own understanding of God, and his listeners understood him in terms of their own perceptions. If he spoke of Father, the listeners formulated their image of father according to their own lights. The New Testament is limited by the people and events that surrounded Jesus of Nazareth, as well as by the limitations of the earliest preachers.

Each author of the gospels understood Jesus differently. In the early preaching, for some who knew Jesus, they compared their appreciation of Jesus as risen Lord to what they had known before. They integrated this new experience with their own understanding of human personality and formulated it in their own way and with their own categories. All of this preaching eventually resulted in a great diversity in the New Testament images of Jesus. The only honest approach to Jesus in the New Testament is to admit that no one biblical portrait exists; there are as many images of Jesus as there are authors and communities that tried to express in writing something of their experience of Jesus.

Works Consulted

Brown, Raymond. *An Introduction to New Testament Christology.* New York/Mahwah, NJ: Paulist Press, 1994.

———. *An Introduction to the New Testament.* New York: Doubleday, 1997.

Cooke, Bernard J. *God's Beloved.* Philadelphia: Trinity Press, 1992.

Crossan, Dominic. *The Historical Jesus.* San Francisco: HarperCollins, 1991.

Jeremias, Joachim. *New Testament Theology.* London: SCM Press, 1971.

Kee, Howard Clark. *What Can We Know About Jesus?* Cambridge, MA: University Press, 1990.

Meier, John. *A Marginal Jew,* vols. I, II, III. New York: Doubleday, 1991, 1994, 2001.

O'Grady, John F. *The Four Gospels and the Jesus Tradition.* New York: Paulist Press, 1989.

———."The Historical Jesus and Christian Faith." *Chicago Studies* 38 (1999): 128– 38.

———. *Models of Jesus Revisited.* New York: Paulist Press, 1994.

Schillebeeckx, Edward. *Jesus: An Experiment in Christology.* New York: Seabury Press, 1979.

Chapter Seven

Jesus in the
Synoptic Gospels

Matthew, Mark, and Luke are called "Synoptics" precisely because they cover the same general themes and teachings of Jesus. Most think that Mark wrote his Gospel first, and then Matthew and Luke had a copy of Mark that they used as a source for their own Gospels. Both Matthew and Luke also had a collection of sayings of Jesus that they incorporated into their efforts to explain to their congregations the meaning of Jesus. Many parallels exist among these three Gospels, but also each one has its own particular approach to Jesus. The one Jesus has many facets. When one facet is portrayed differently than the other, the usual reason lies with the needs of the community.

Jesus in the Gospel of Mark

Each evangelist's perspective flowed from the needs of a particular audience. Each presents a view of Jesus that was not meant to be exclusive or exhaustive. Only when the richness of this variety of approaches to Jesus is understood can anyone begin to appreciate the impact that Jesus had on people. The Gospel of Mark was probably written in Rome around the year 70 for a mixed community of Jewish and Gentile Christians who had

99

trouble dealing with suffering and accepting faith in a crucified Messiah. They also were experiencing persecution.

The Gospel of Mark has no infancy narrative and seems to locate Jesus' divine sonship in his baptism. Jesus is first and foremost the suffering Son of Man who must die. On three occasions Mark has Jesus give a prediction of his passion: Mark 8:31, 9:31, and 10:33–34. The general theology that pervades the Gospel of Mark focuses on the fate of those who are faithful to God. They hear the Word of God and preach it; they are rejected and are delivered up. John the Baptist preaches and he is delivered up (Mark 1:14); Jesus preaches and is delivered up (Mark 9:30; 13:33); the disciples preach and they too are delivered up (Mark 13:9). Death appears to be the fate of all.

Whatever happened to Jesus will also happen to his followers. It is a sad Gospel in many ways, filled with misunderstandings on the part of the disciples, and with pain inflicted on Jesus as he is abandoned by family and friends and eventually by the entire population. Mark wishes to speak about Jesus, but only in relationship to the sufferings that are part of the Christian experience. Jesus as the suffering Son of Man is the model for all who would be disciples.

The Death of Jesus

However central the death of Jesus is to Mark's Gospel, it is not his sole concern. The author also tells how Jesus lived. In presenting Jesus' way of suffering and his rejection, Mark always places it within the context of the life of Jesus as one who serves. The climax of his teaching on suffering thus includes his way of living: "The Son of Man came not to be served but to serve, and to give his life as a ransom for many" (Mark 10:45). The author presents the cross not so much as an atonement for sin, but as the result of obedience to the law of God in life. God mysteriously wills that the Son must suffer and die, so the Son willingly accepts his fate: "...the Son of man must suffer..." (Mark 8:31). Jesus is patterned after the righteous sufferer in Psalm 22:

My God, my God why have you abandoned me?...
Yet you are holy,
   enthroned on the praises of Israel,...
you kept me safe upon my mother's breasts....
Be not far from me, for trouble is near and there is none
     to help. (Ps 22:1, 3, 9, 11)

Jesus is the model for others in his living and dying, but his actual death offers the deepest insight into Mark's Christology. The death of Jesus on the cross lays open a quality of life which patterns what true life means for all people. The authentic follower of Jesus must take up the cross daily and follow the Lord. No optional road, no substitute, and no other means exist by which a person can be a disciple. The believers are sad as they experience persecution, but they are also filled with the hope directed toward sharing in the glorification of the Son of Man. For Mark, the cross and suffering stand always in the foreground, but the resurrection remains in the background as the foundation for hope. As the Son of Man must suffer and die and then rise, so he offers the same hope to those who will follow him. The glorified Lord will bring his faithful followers to share in his glory. Mark understood Jesus only in terms of the suffering Messiah, who asks his disciples to join with him and share in his sufferings so that all can share in his glory. To a persecuted community, Mark offered consolation by reminding them that all who will follow a thorn-crowned Lord must expect to share in his pain before they can enter into his glory.

The Son of Man in Mark

The phrase "Son of Man" can mean simply *man* in a generic sense, as found in Psalm 8:4: "...what is man that you are mindful of him or the Son of Man that you care for him?" This also may have been the meaning in the pre-Markan tradition as found in Mark 2:28: "...so the Son of man is lord even of the sabbath." The original meaning may have been that everyone makes decisions

Men in the Bible

with regard to the rightful observance of the Sabbath since the Sabbath was made for all and not vice versa. The use of "man" and "son of man" stand in parallelism. The original meaning of the story of the disciples going through the fields of standing grain may have been an effort on the part of Jesus to give "man," simply as a human being, authority over the Sabbath. No doubt, however, in Mark this meaning at most underlies the more important thought that Jesus, as the "Son of Man," is actually "Lord" of the Sabbath.

Jesus himself alone uses the title in the gospel, and always in the presence of his disciples or the inner circle of Peter, James, and John. Whether Jesus ever actually used the title himself and associated it with dying and rising remains unknown. In the Gospel of Mark, however, this theme predominates. Throughout Mark's Gospel, the title refers to Jesus as the one who was betrayed (14:21); arrested (14:41); who suffered (9:12); died (10:45); who was raised from the dead (9:9); who was seated at God's right hand in heaven (14:26); and who would come at the end of the age to collect the faithful into the kingdom of God (13:26). Jesus is human in the use of this title, but also more than human.

The Power of Jesus in Word and Miracle

The preaching and teaching of Jesus, as well as his power to work miracles, form the foundation for the whole meaning of Jesus in the Gospel of Mark. The heart of the Gospel may be the suffering Son of Man, but the activity of the Son of Man must also be understood to enter into the fuller meaning of the good news according to Mark.

The Gospel almost begins with a reference to preaching: "Jesus came into Galilee, preaching the gospel of God...." (Mark1:14). This opening chapter ends with a sense of compulsion. Jesus had to go about the land preaching (Mark 1:38). Mark does not dwell, however, on the actual content of the preaching of Jesus. Even when Jesus sent out his disciples to preach, he does not mention precisely what they were to preach (Mark 6:12). He speaks only of repentance that repeats the actual preaching of Jesus in Mark 1:15, and the very content of the preaching of John the Baptizer in Mark 1:4.

Teacher

Jesus often functions as a teacher of the law, a "rabbi." In Mark 10:17 a man asks Jesus about eternal life and Jesus reacts out of the tradition of the law, just as a rabbi or scribe might react. People, whether friend or foe, also address Jesus as a teacher (Mark 9:38; 10:35; 12:14, 19, 32; 13:1). He taught in the synagogue, beside the sea, or wherever crowds would gather. Also, Jesus identifies his ministry with teaching: "Day by day I was with you in the temple teaching…" (Mark 14:49). He also used the title *teacher* when he instructed his disciples to prepare the Passover: The Teacher says, "Where is my guest room, where I am to eat the Passover with my disciples?" (Mark 14:14).

Mark saw teaching as a regular activity of Jesus and when the disciples return from their preaching journey they narrate not only what they had done but also what they had taught (Mark 6:30), even though they were not instructed to teach (Mark 6:7, 12, 13). For Mark, if Jesus taught, then his disciples had to teach just as his church would teach. The combination of the teaching activity of Jesus and of the church appears clearly in the parables. Mark saw the parables as a principal way in which Jesus taught, and then the church could use the parables in its own teaching. As a result, many of the parables were embellished by the early church as they sought new meaning in the teachings of Jesus, and as they tried to apply the parables to the present situation of the followers of Jesus.

Miracle Worker

In addition to Jesus as a teacher, the author of the second Gospel also preserved the traditions about Jesus as a miracle worker. The ancient world teemed with magicians and wonder workers. Both Jews and Greeks had their share of those people associated with marvelous deeds. Rabbis healed the sick, conquered evil spirits, and even made ugly women beautiful. The Greek world had its magicians and devotees of gods who made the lame walk, the blind see. Jesus' performing miracles does not set him apart from many of his contemporaries. To work a miracle does not in itself attest to the identity of the presence of God's envoy, or the one who would inaugurate the kingdom of God. Even the miracles themselves, as performed by Jesus, are open to various interpretations. Reading the miracles of Jesus from a personal perspective, they appear to be signs of the presence of God with him. To his opponents, however, they were proof that he must be destroyed because he was involved with the power of evil: "He is possessed by Beelzebul and by the prince of demons he casts out the demons" (Mark 3:22). Even his family thought he was mad after they witnessed his deeds of power: "And when his own heard it, they went out to seize him for they said, he is mad" (Mark 3:21). With such a mixed background, the survival of the miracle stories in the early tradition is itself a marvel. Better to concentrate on what Jesus taught and avoid the ambiguity of the miraculous was in fact the tact of some of the fathers of the church. But for Mark, this was not the solution. Evidently Jesus did perform miracles and if they could be ambiguous, Mark decided to preserve the stories and give them his own interpretation, or at least the interpretation of his community. Mark adapted and interpreted miracle stories as he had adapted and interpreted the teaching of Jesus to suit the needs of the early church. Both were sharpened and showed Jesus powerful in word and in miracle in his public ministry.

For Mark, Jesus still lived in the church in Rome; he was equally powerful in word and deed for those who, through their faith in him, joined themselves into a fellowship of people whose Lord he would always remain. Jesus, in the Gospel of Mark, is the suffering Son of Man, the model for all believers, who gave his life for others, powerful in word and in miracles.

Jesus in the Gospel of Matthew

Composed in the seventies, probably at Antioch for a mixed community of Jewish and Gentile Christians, Matthew begins his Gospel by carefully presenting Jesus as both Son of David and Son of Abraham (Matt 1:1). The one foretold of old now fulfills all of the expectations of Israel; in him all of the nations of the world are blessed. Jesus stands prominently in this Gospel as a great authoritative and ethical teacher, part of the tradition of Israel. Like the great leader, Moses, Jesus gives clear guidance and direction to his people. He inaugurates the kingdom of God and, as the final agent of God, he consummates God's purpose in the world (Mark 5:17–18). Jesus, in Matthew's Gospel, is the founder of the New Israel, the church, that brings to fulfillment all of the ancient expectations. Matthew has a peculiar interest in the Old Testament and frequently refers to Old Testament prophecies that are accomplished in Jesus. In the infancy narrative alone, five times he refers to the Old Testament and uses the passages to demonstrate that Jesus fulfills Israel's hopes as foretold by the prophets.

The Christology of Matthew

As teacher, Jesus' authority commanded respect in Mark (Mark 1:27) but Matthew is more interested in giving the content of this teaching in the Sermon on the Mount (Matt 5:1—7:29). Matthew systematizes the teaching of Jesus into a unified body. This tendency agrees with the general tone of the Gospel which presents a community that is clearly organized. The author tries, in fact, to present as orderly a teaching on ethics as can be found in the Old Testament.

Apologetical overtones are heard throughout the Gospel, especially in the infancy narratives and in the passion account. These two sections would have been of special interest to Jewish converts, and so Matthew relates the experiences of Jesus in both instances to the Old Testament. He demonstrates that, in truth,

Jesus is the Messiah of Israel, and offers explanations that he hopes will convince his readers that the Messiah had to suffer.

Following the general pattern developed in Mark, Matthew presents the fundamental messiahship of Jesus but nuances its meaning. He alone among the Synoptics adds to Peter's confession of Jesus as the Messiah, "the Son of the living God" (Matt 16:16). He alone gives the injunction against the sword at the time of Jesus' arrest, which indicates for him that Jesus was not the political and apocalyptic figure of popular messianic expectation (Matt 26:52).

Matthew also deals with the theme of the suffering servant, but has a distinctive way of portraying this element of his Christology. Mark interprets Jesus' mission in light of the suffering servant by subtle overtones, while Matthew actually identifies Jesus with this figure from Deutero-Isaiah. The author of Matthew's Gospel seems to perceive more deeply the mission of Jesus to be the servant of all and bear the suffering of his passion and death for the sake of the many.

More so than in any of the other gospels, Matthew also presents Jesus as Lord. Even when Satan, in the temptation narrative, approaches Jesus, he does so with the reverence due the Lord. A sense of adoration pervades his ministry, from the adoration of the Magi to Peter falling down and confessing his belief in Jesus as Lord (Matt 2:11; 14:33). That Jesus is the Son of God in a most unusual way, Matthew demonstrates in the story of his origin, and exemplifies in his ministry. He has authority and power and commands a sense of awe and adoration. As the Lord, he teaches with authority and gives specific directions to all who will come after him. Finally, as the eschatological Lord, Jesus lives in his church until the end of time (Matt 28:17–20). The Christology of Matthew develops further insights into the meaning of Jesus by presenting him not only as the fulfillment of the Old Law, but especially as the divine lawgiver, the exalted Lord, worthy of worship, present always in the church. He suffers, but his suffering pales in light of the meaning of his Lordship.

Old Testament Influence

Because the community was composed of Jews and Gentiles, the author anxiously preserved the old from Judaism and added the new from Christianity. The genealogy places Jesus in the line of David and the author finds parallels throughout the Old Testament, even in places where no one else might see the relationship. Every word of the Old Testament that might have prophetic significance for Jesus, Matthew seems to discover and incorporates into his Gospel. Perhaps an early member of the Jewish Christian community gathered together possible references to Jesus from Jewish writings and Matthew used this collection as a source for his Gospel. The suffering servant of Isaiah is the servant of the Lord of the Gospel who himself has borne our afflictions and carried our sorrows: This was to fulfill what was spoken by the prophet Isaiah, "He took our infirmities and bore our diseases" (Matt 8:17). The proclamation of Hosea, "...out of Egypt I have called my son" (Hos 11:1), although referring to the Exodus of the Israelites, becomes for Matthew a renewal of the ancient history of Israel in the Son of Man.

The Jewish character is also evident in the attitude of Jesus toward the Law of Moses. It almost seems as if the Law remains in force without any modification. Some Jewish Christians in the community of Matthew would be anxious to continue the observance of the Law, and they would find sure foundation in the words of Jesus recorded by Matthew:

> "Think not that I have come to abolish the law and the prophets; I have come not to abolish them but to fulfill them." (Matt 5:17)

Possibly to respond to the needs of his Gentile Christians, Matthew also records the two-fold commandment of love of God and neighbor, and then adds: On these two commandments depend all the law and the prophets (Matt 22:40). The Old Testament is the background for the Jesus of Matthew, but not without a sense of an opening to the Gentiles. Jesus fulfills the Old Testament but the emphasis remains on the fulfillment. The power of the Old Testament tradition affects every major aspect of the life of Jesus. The Old Testament creates the history and milieu out of which Matthew creates his portrait of Jesus.

The Exalted Son of God

In the first four chapters of Matthew he treats the person of Jesus and acknowledges that he is both son of David and son of Abraham, but preeminently Jesus is the exalted Son of God. Conceived by the power of God, he will shepherd God's people (Matt 2:6) and prove himself in confrontation with Satan (Matt 4:3–10). But for Matthew, Jesus is not Son of God in the manner of ancient kings, or angels, or even the just. Instead Jesus is the Son of God who will be raised and will reign with God with all authority in heaven and on earth (Matt 28:18).

> And Jesus came and said to them, "All authority in heaven and on earth has been given to me. Go therefore and make disciples of all nations, baptizing them in the name of the Father and of the Son and of the Holy Spirit, teaching them to observe all that I have commanded you; and lo, I am with you always, to the close of the age." (Matt 28:18–20)

As Son of God, Jesus enjoys a unique relationship with the Father and has been chosen by God to be the exclusive representative among peoples. He shares in the divine authority and confronts his listeners and so reveals the Father to whomever he wills. As Son of God, Jesus acknowledges his election by God by living in complete fellowship with God, and relying upon God totally by being perfectly obedient to God's will. The so-called Johannine thunderbolt in Matthew expresses this relationship well:

> All things have been delivered to me by my Father; and no one knows the Son except the Father, and no one

knows the Father except the Son and any one to whom the Son chooses to reveal him. (Matt 11:27)

In the second part of his Gospel (Matt 4:17—16:20), Matthew fills out the meaning of the Son of Man by explaining his ministry of teaching and healing. In the third part of the Gospel (Matt 16:21—28:30), Jesus as Son moves toward death and fulfillment in the resurrection. The Sanhedrin condemns Jesus for claiming divine sonship (Matt 26:63–66); he is ridiculed as the Son of God by the people (Matt 27:39–40), and dies upon the cross trusting completely in God his Father (Matt 27:38–54). But God will not allow the Son to experience eternal defeat. God raised him up:

> He is not here; for he has risen, as he said. Come, see the place where he lay. Then go quickly and tell his disciples that he has risen from the dead, and behold, he is going before you to Galilee; there you will see him. Lo, I have told you. (Matt 28:6–7)

God exalted him to absolute and universal authority in heaven and on earth (Matt 28:18–20). Now others will be empowered by the Spirit of God to make disciples of all nations, assured of the abiding presence of the Son of God until the end of the age. The title *Son of God* appears at his conception, birth and infancy, baptism and temptations, public ministry, death, resurrection, and exaltation. It expresses for Matthew the mystery of the person of Jesus as Messiah and represents an exalted confession of the Matthean Christian community.

Messiah as Teacher

The ministry of Jesus in Matthew's Gospel emphasizes his teaching. He teaches the new covenant much as Moses was the teacher of the old covenant. He has the boldness to proclaim: "You have heard that it was said to the men of old...but I say to you..." (Matt 5:21–22). In the eyes of the Jews, Jesus blasphemed by such a claim to authority. As the new teacher he claims an authority that intrinsically requires no credentials other than the obvious rightness and truth of his declarations. He truly speaks about God in a new way and, although he often seems to be a new Moses in his teaching, he also seems to teach as God taught Moses. Unlike the scribes, he teaches with authority and the people recognize that a prophet has risen in the land:

> And when Jesus finished these sayings, the crowds were astonished at his teaching, for he taught them as one who has authority, and not as their scribes. (Matt 7:28–29)

Not only does he teach, but he lives what he proclaims. The teacher of new ideas remains relatively harmless unless the teacher puts these new ideas into practice. Jesus lived what he taught. He has a devotion to the Law but interprets this Law based on the criteria of love of God and love of neighbor. The scribes and the Pharisees frequently offered interpretations of the Law but never in the radical way in which Jesus taught and lived. Whatever helped in the fulfillment of the command of love of God and neighbor must be practiced. Whatever hindered these commands, especially the love of neighbor, must be ignored. Love founds all law and love alone is the principle by which the Law of Moses must be interpreted and judged (Matt 22:34–39). For Jesus, love meant an unlimited and unconditional willingness to serve. This command he lived personally and he called all of his followers to do likewise.

The great teacher proclaimed a new approach to God based upon love, but not without its pain. The ancient Law of Deuteronomy promised, for the most part, material blessings of harvest and fertility of cattle, many children, and a long life. Jesus also proclaims a blessing to his followers but one which involves a commitment to an ideal, to the kingdom of God. They will renounce personal rights and privileges and willingly serve and endure persecution, even unto death, for the name of the Lord.

Healer

Matthew also presents Jesus as a healer. Jesus knows the need for physical healing. The exalted Son of God and great teacher touches people with compassion. He overpowers the forces of evil that threaten human society and brings wholeness. In four chapters Matthew gathers together the miracle stories about Jesus: chapters 8, 9, 12, and 14. Most of these miraculous events appear also in Mark, but here, in Matthew, they are often abbreviated to emphasize the essential elements: the person in faith recognizes that Jesus makes manifest the saving power of God. Miracles result from faith; they reveal the healing effects of God's grace that has been given to the individual because of the person's faith in Jesus. Faith heals the woman with the hemorrhage (Matt 9:18–22); two blind men see because of their faith (Matt 9:27–31). The miracle collection in Matthew 14:13—15:39 parallels the miracles of Mark 6–8 with such important miracles as the feeding of the crowds, the walking on the water, and the healing of the daughter of the Canaanite woman. Here Matthew, unlike Mark, used the miracles to invite the people to follow Jesus in faith. In the narrative of the walking on the water in Matthew, the disciples fall down in worship (Matt 14:33). In Mark, the disciples do not understand for their hearts are hardened (Mark 6:53–56). Jesus bears God's message of compassion and healing and those who believe, who recognize the saving presence of God in Jesus, are restored to life.

Kurios *(Lord)*

The title *Kurios* is significant in the First Gospel. It occurs on the lips of persons who address Jesus in faith, the only exception being the accursed in the last judgment scene in chapter 25:37. The title has a confessional character. Most often Matthew used this title to attribute divine authority and an exalted station to Jesus

(Matt 8:2, 6, 8, 25; 14:28, etc.). The usage, however, was more from the Matthean community than the actual time of the ministry of Jesus. In Matthew 8:25 the disciples in the boat seek the help of the sleeping Jesus and call out: "Save us, Lord; we are perishing." The same scene in Mark has the title "Teacher" (Mark 4:38). No doubt Matthew used this Greek expression to denote the exalted position of Jesus, the one close to God, for the title is also used to translate the sacred Hebrew name of God into Greek. *Kurios* was used by the Matthean community in worship and prayer, as well as the title used for the second coming of Jesus in glory. Matthew projects the use of the title backwards to the ministry of Jesus, for he knows that Jesus now lives as exalted Lord of all.

Jesus as Lord of All

Combining all of the titles of Jesus—such as Son of God, Son of David, Son of Abraham, Emmanuel, *Messiah*, Son of Man, *Kurios*—forms an image of Jesus as the divine and exalted one from God who has returned to God, and who has taught and healed as the manifestation of the loving God in human history. Jesus is the presence of the transcendent God and, thus, demands worship and adoration. He is also the sign of the closeness of a compassionate God through his power to heal.

Many times readers of Matthew note that he lacks the vigor and detail of Mark, but his Gospel has a dignity which has made it the source for centuries of preaching on the person of Jesus. Nowhere is this more evident than in the conclusion. This ending of the Gospel (Matt 28:16–20) may well be the Matthean summary of the resurrection proclamation rather than the actual words of Jesus. Any believer of the second or third generation also might have used these words to express what it meant to be a Christian. Whatever the origin of the conclusion, the true believer knows that all authority and power had been given to Jesus.

In his ministry Jesus had transformed the lives of women and men and had drawn them away from a life of sin and self-concern into the fellowship of a new creation. Where once people had been divided and separated, now they were united in a common faith. Only a person of extraordinary power could have accomplished such a task. Even the limitations on the relationship between God and people of the old dispensation have disappeared. God has exalted Jesus as Lord. Now the church, as the community of believers, could go out into the world and proclaim the sovereignty of Jesus as Lord of *all*. The resurrection and exaltation has made permanent and universally available the presence of the Master. That presence in the church as exalted Lord and Son of God was the pledge of victory and of the ultimate fulfillment of the plan of God for *all*. The Jesus of Matthew's Gospel inspires awe and worship, gives guidance and direction, and assures the presence of a kind and compassionate God who is ever willing to respond to the human world of suffering, conflict, and pain. Jesus is God with us.

Jesus in the Gospel of Luke

The Gospel of Luke presents an entirely different picture of Jesus. No longer Mark's suffering Son of Man, nor the powerful Teacher and Lord of Matthew, Jesus is seen here as the kind and compassionate savior, filled with the Spirit of God and endowed with the gift of effectively preaching the Word of God. Jesus' appearance in the synagogue in Nazareth early in Luke's Gospel sets the tone for what follows. Jesus as the teacher is invested with the power of the Spirit. He fulfills in himself the prophecy of Isaiah: "The spirit of the Lord is upon me.... Today this scripture has been fulfilled in your hearing" (Luke 4:18a, 21). In his ministry people are impressed by his authority (Luke 31, 36–37). He shows his power in his deeds, for he is not only the messenger of the kingdom, but also its messianic agent who reveals the eschatological reign of God through how he acts. This confluence of word and deed gives him power over the forces of evil. Thus he banishes Satan in the course of his ministry (Luke 4:39) and subjects evil spirits to himself (Luke 4:36); he cures by his word (Luke 4:39), and in his role as the teacher he heals (Luke 5:17–26; 6:6–11).

The Gospel of Joy and Mercy

Written probably in the eighties to a predominantly Gentile community, Luke offers a Gospel of great joy. Jesus brings blessedness to all who respond to him in faith. At his birth the angels proclaim a message of joy for all (Luke 2:11); Jesus rejoices at the return of his disciples from preaching (Luke 10:20); and God rejoices over one sinner who repents (Luke 15:10). The Christology of Luke captures the mercy and compassion of Jesus. The fifteenth chapter is often called "the gospel within the gospel" for in it Luke presents three central parables: the lost sheep, the lost coin, and the prodigal (lost) son. In each instance the story illustrates the mercy and forgiveness of God and the joy over a sinner who repents and returns. His compassion extends to the outcasts of society, calling them to be his friends. Shepherds, outcasts themselves, welcomed him at his birth. The same pattern continues throughout his ministry. Sinners are always welcome; tax collectors, prostitutes, and anyone else who feels left out can find company with Jesus as the forgiving savior.

Prayer

Luke also portrays Jesus as a man of prayer. He prayed just before his baptism (Luke 3:21). After he worked miracles he withdrew to pray (Luke 5:16). He prayed all night before choosing his disciples (Luke 6:12) and prayed after the miracle of the loaves (Luke 9:18). Jesus prayed as a prelude to the transfiguration (Luke 9:28–29), and was praying when his disciples asked him to teach them to pray (Luke 11:1). He prayed in the garden (Luke 22:39–45) and from the cross (Luke 23:46). By Luke's account, Jesus always remains in close contact with God.

Universalism

Jesus has a universal interest in Luke's Gospel. In his prayer Simeon joins together Israel and the pagan world as recipients of the salvation that Jesus brings (Luke 2:31–32). Jesus, in Luke, calls a Roman centurion and a Samaritan leper models of faith (Luke

7:9; 17:19). Luke also emphasizes the concern of Jesus for women. Jesus treats women with a special compassion. He heals the woman with a hemorrhage (Luke 8:43–48), cares for a woman who is a sinner (Luke 7:36–50), responds to the need of the widow of Naim (Luke 7:11–17)—and women provide for him (Luke 23:55).

Jesus and God His Father

This same Gospel deals with the special relationship that existed between Jesus and God his Father. He is the Son of God (Luke 3:22; 22:29; 24:49) and, like Matthew, Luke has his version of the so-called Johannine thunderbolt in the Synoptic tradition:

> Everything has been given to me by my Father. No one knows the Son except the Father and no one knows the Father except the Son and anyone to whom the Son wishes to reveal him. (Luke 10:22)

At his baptism God declared Jesus as Son, but previously in the infancy narrative his very conception was an act of God, making him the Son of the Most High (Luke 1:32). The father who gives Jesus his mission of salvation has decreed all (Luke 22:22) and has given Jesus the Spirit to fulfill this mission. Finally, after Jesus has been raised up by the Father, he too can send the Spirit (Luke 24:49ff., Acts 1:1ff.).

The Human and Divine Jesus

Jesus is a Jew, born in Bethlehem (Luke 2:6–7) of Davidic lineage (Luke 11:2; 2:4; 3:31), and raised in Nazareth (Luke 4:16). He was a man attested by God with mighty works (Acts 2:22). The Lukan Jesus is very human, filled with emotion. He responds to the widow of Naim (Luke 7:13), enjoys human friendships with Martha and Mary, and eats with friends and even with sinners. He shares a meal with Levi (Luke 5:29) and with Zacchaeus (Luke 19:5). He seems to enjoy life and when faced with death, prays:

Father, if you are willing, remove this cup from me; nevertheless, not my will but your will be done. (Luke 22:42)

The same dying Jesus will pray to God: "Father, into your hands I commend my spirit" (Luke 23:46). Jesus is the kind and compassionate savior, filled with human needs and emotions, who responds to people in a warm and forgiving manner. Jesus also lives and dies the faithful one of God and always in a human manner.

Luke also presents the Jesus who transcends the human condition. His conception is through the power of the Spirit (Luke 1:34–35). The Spirit controls his ministry (Luke 3:22; 4:1, 14, 18; 10:21). He has a special relationship to God as his Father (Luke 2:49; 3:22; 9:35; 10:21–22; 23:46). Finally, through his resurrection he becomes Lord and Messiah through the power of God (Acts 2:24, 32; 3:15; 4:10; 5:30; 10:40). Each of these elements, taken together with the human dimension of Jesus, comprises Lukan Christology. The very human Jesus goes beyond the dimension of humanity and lives and acts in the divine realm without losing the human. Luke connects the human and the divine after the resurrection with his insistence on the importance of the ascension.

Luke and History

Unlike the other evangelists, Luke divides the time after the death of Jesus into set periods. God raised Jesus from the dead on the third day. The other evangelists end here. Then Luke adds forty days until the time when he ascends into heaven to sit at the right hand of God (Acts 2:33; 5:31). Then another ten days pass before the disciples experience the coming of the Spirit on Pentecost. Luke presents ministry, death, resurrection, ascension, and exaltation and, finally, the coming of the Spirit as the culmination of the meaning of Jesus. Chronology figures prominently in his theology. Luke has had so much of an influence on Christianity, that the church uses his time frame for liturgical celebrations. The Easter season continues with the celebration of the ascension forty days after Easter and then Pentecost completes the cycle, ten days after the ascension. None of the other gospels have such a division. The Gospel of Luke ends with a veiled reference to the ascending of Jesus (Luke 24:50) and the Acts of the Apostles opens with Jesus ascending (Acts 1:9–11).

Kurios *(Lord)*

Luke used the title *Lord* most frequently for Jesus in both of his books. He used it for both God and Jesus. Pre-Christian Palestinian Jews did on occasion refer to God as Lord, and it was generally used as a Greek substitute for the sacred name of God. Jewish Christians, probably the Hellenists, used the formula in reference to Jesus as a response to the earliest preaching. Such a usage would put Jesus on the same level as God, but without identifying him with God. Luke will refer to God as *Abba,* for example, but never will address Jesus as Abba. Jesus is Son. In the words of Peter, God the Father made Jesus Lord through his resurrection:

> Let all the house of Israel therefore know assuredly that God has made him both Lord and Christ, this Jesus whom you crucified. (Acts 2:36)

In the public ministry of Jesus, Luke, like Matthew, has retrojected this title and has even used the title in the origin of Jesus. The angels announce to the shepherds that "Christ the Lord" is born in Bethlehem (Luke 2:11). In so doing, Luke has recorded the usage in the early Christian communities, which saw Jesus on a par with God. The title *Lord* as used by Luke connotes his otherness or his transcendent character, but not necessarily in a philosophical and metaphysical sense. The title, rather, expresses the influence that the resurrection has had on the followers of Jesus. For them, because Jesus has been raised, he has been elevated to the throne of God. Once Luke and the Christian community accepted this position of Jesus, Luke could read back into the ministry of Jesus an awareness of his proximity to God.

Christ/Messiah

Although not used as frequently as *Lord,* the title of *Christ* or *Messiah* becomes the most important title for Luke in his two-volume work. Luke preaches salvation and Jesus the anointed one of God brings this salvation. The Gospel almost closes with the question posed by the risen Jesus: "Was not the Christ bound to suffer all this before entering into his glory?" (Luke 24:26). And, it is Luke alone who tells us that the followers of Jesus were called *Christians* (Acts 11:26; 26:28).

Sometimes the title may be translated as *Christ* to suit the Gentile audience of Luke, and at other times it is translated as *Messiah,* conveying its basic meaning as one anointed by God, for the Jewish audience. For modern believers the title has become almost the second name for Jesus and even in Luke, something similar has already taken place (Acts 2:38; 3:6; 4:10, and so on).

In its Old Testament usage, the title *Messiah* (the anointed one) referred to certain historical persons chosen and anointed by God for the service of God's people. The kings of Israel were anointed. Also, at times, the high priest was God's anointed. Even the Persian King Cyrus was the anointed of God destined to return the people to their land (Isa 45:1).

At the time of Jesus, *messiah* indicated either someone sent by God in the kingly Davidic and political tradition, or someone in the priestly tradition. The political overtones for the title would have been known to Jesus and his followers. This would account for the Lukan and Matthean correction when Jesus admitted to a messianic role as attested before the high priest in the Gospel of Mark:

> Again the high priest asked him, "Are you the Christ,
> the Son of the Blessed?" And Jesus said, "I am; and you
> will see the Son of man seated at the right hand of

Power, and coming with the clouds of heaven." (Mark 14:61–62)

Both Matthew and Luke present the same scene with a refusal on the part of Jesus to respond: "If I tell you, you will not believe; and if I ask you, you will not answer" (Luke 22:67b–68).

After his death and resurrection, the title *Christ* or *Messiah* became a principal title for Jesus in the Lukan writings. Jesus was crucified as "King of the Jews" (Luke 23:38), but for his followers he became the Messiah. Within a few years after his death, Christians began to use *Jesus Christ, Christ Jesus,* or *Jesus the Messiah* as honorific designations that suited Jesus alone. Jesus is God's anointed agent announcing a new form of salvation to humankind.

Savior

A third title important for Luke is *Savior.* The title actually occurs only once in the Gospel (Luke 2:11), and occasionally in Acts. The meaning of salvation, however, takes on a particular significance for Luke. The author of the Third Gospel presents Jesus as one who brings salvation to the world as its great benefactor. The title itself was used frequently in the Greco-Roman world applied to gods, philosophers, physicians, kings, and emperors. In the Old Testament it is used for individuals whom God had raised up for the deliverance of the people, as well as for God as the giver of salvation (1 Sam 10:19; Isa 45:15, 21). The Christian use of the title may be influenced by both traditions. In the gospels the meaning of savior denotes deliverance from such evils as sickness, infirmity, or sin. In Acts it denotes the complete process: the effect of Jesus on human history and humankind. It is not just deliverance but the actual experience of God's presence in love, seeking out what was lost and bringing the lost home.

Conclusion

For Luke, Jesus lived as the kind and compassionate Savior. He does not offend. He responds to all in need and offers kindness to specific people. This Savior, filled with the Spirit, frequently turned to his Father in prayer. All of the titles used by Luke support this fundamental meaning of Jesus. He came to bring salvation, God's saving presence, to humankind, and accomplished this precisely because of his unique relationship to God and his possession of the Spirit. Luke makes Jesus most attractive to all, calling all to accept the saving presence of God, especially those in need. The poor, the outcast, the neglected, the marginalized—all find welcome and comfort in the Jesus of the Gospel of Luke. Since most people feel left out, at least sometimes in life, a kind and compassionate friend who reaches out to invite everyone inside makes the hurt disappear. The Jesus of Luke is everyone's friend.

Topics for Discussion

1. How is Jesus as "Son of Man unto Death" in Mark related to contemporary Christianity?

2. Mark adds a mysterious character to his image of Jesus. Why?

3. Does Mark have trouble understanding that Jesus is human?

4. Does Mark have trouble relating divinity to Jesus?

5. What is Mark's fundamental image of Jesus and how does it make sense today?

6. Jesus is a great teacher and the Lord, and has many other titles in Matthew. How do they fit together in the theology of Matthew?

7. Matthew presents Jesus as present in all people in need (25:31–46). Is this a good model for today?

8. Matthew presents Jesus as Lord of all who gives guidance and direction to the church. How does this image help?

9. Do you like the Jesus in the Gospel of Matthew?

10. Luke portrays Jesus as kind and compassionate. Is this his basic model of Jesus?

11. What appeals to people in the Jesus in the Gospel of Luke?

12. Jesus prays frequently in this Gospel. Is this part of the appeal and is this important in understanding Jesus?

13. Compare the model of Luke with the model of Matthew.

Works Consulted

Jesus in Mark

Carroll, W. "The Jesus of Mark's Gospel." *The Bible Today* 103 (1979): 2105–112.

Donahue, J. "Jesus as the Parable of God in the Gospel of Mark." *Interpretation* 32 (1978): 369–86.

Lambrecht, J. "The Christology of Mark." *Biblical Theology Bulletin* 3 (1973): 256–73.

Matera, Frank. *New Testament Christology.* Louisville, KY: Westminster John Knox, 1999.

Richard, Earl. *Jesus: One and Many.* Wilmington, DE: Glazier, 1988.

Schnackenburg, Rudolf. *Jesus in the Gospels.* Louisville, KY: Westminster John Knox, 1995.

Jesus in Matthew

Buckley, Thomas. "The Christology of Matthew." *Chicago Studies* 40 (2001): 251–60.

Gaston, E. "The Messiah of Israel as Teacher of the Gentiles." *Interpretation* 29 (1975): 24–40.

Kingsbury, Jack. *Matthew: Structure, Christology, Kingdom.* Philadelphia: Fortress Press, 1975.

Matera, Frank. *New Testament Christology.* Louisville, KY: Westminster John Knox, 1999.

Meier, John P. *The Vision of Matthew: Christ, Church, and Morality in the First Gospel.* New York: Paulist Press, 1979.

Richard, Earl. *Jesus: One and Many.* Wilmington, DE: Glazier, 1988.

Schnackenburg, Rudolf. *Jesus in the Gospels.* Louisville, KY: Westminster John Knox, 1995.

Jesus in Luke

Fitzmyer, Joseph. *Luke the Theologian: Aspects of His Teaching.* New York/Mahwah, NJ: Paulist Press, 1989.

Matera, Frank. *New Testament Christology.* Louisville, KY: Westminster John Knox, 1999.

Orton, David, ed. *The Composition of Luke's Gospel.* Boston: Brill, 1999.

Richard, Earl. *Jesus: One and Many.* Wilmington, DE: Glazier, 1988.

Schnackenburg, Rudolf. *Jesus in the Gospels.* Louisville, KY: Westminster John Knox, 1995.

Chapter Eight

Jesus in the Gospel of John

The Gospel of John differs significantly from the Synoptic Gospels in the portrayal of Jesus. In the past, many scholars have searched for the key to the Jesus in John. They studied the titles; they explored the relationship between the human and the divine, history and faith, person and function. But these same scholars never seem to have agreed on a single key. One possible approach focuses on relating Jesus to his followers and, in addition, John clearly emphasizes the divinity of Jesus. He begins his Gospel with a hymn to the Word, which relates the eternal Word to the historical Jesus (John 1:13). The theology of the prologue relates this Word not only to the incarnation and to God, but also to the meaning of creation and to the response expected from those who hear this Word (John 1:12). Along with this sense of divinity comes the awareness that the divine finds resolution in a human response. Then the meaning of Jesus is complete.

Jesus is also preeminently Son in this Gospel, where the close relationship that exists between Jesus and the Father is constantly emphasized; but he is also the son of Joseph (John 1:45). As Son, Jesus calls people to believe in him, to recognize him as the presence of the Father (John 14:9). Jesus, the incarnation of the preexistent Word, always speaks from eternity. He knows the secrets of people's hearts. He knows all that will happen to him, and yet allows the drama to be played out. Jesus is divine in this Gospel, not only in his baptism, his resurrection, and his birth, but also prior to all these events. He was with God and, as Word, was God.

The Divine/Human Jesus

Scholars and readers have long recognized that the Fourth Gospel portrays a divine Jesus. It begins with a hymn celebrating the preexistent Word of God, related to God with a closeness of persons: "...the word was with God and the word was God" (John 1:1). The word became flesh as Son but never left the bosom of the Father: ...the only Son who is in the bosom of the Father, he has made him known (John 1:18). As Jesus of Nazareth, the Word became flesh, and possessed supernatural knowledge. He cured with a word (John 4:50), changed water into wine (John 2:7–9), gave life through his word to Lazarus (John 11:43). He never suffered. With a sereneness that astonished all, he controlled his passion from the moment of arrest to his final proclamation that it was finished.

The contrast to the Synoptics makes evident the emphasis on the divinity of Jesus in this Gospel. In the earlier gospels Jesus does not know everything. He grows in wisdom and grace (Luke 2:52); appears to be ignorant of the final day (Mark 13:32); suffers a painful agony (Luke 22:40–42), and cries out from the cross: "My God, my God, why hast thou forsaken me?" (Mark 15:34; Matt 27:46). Jesus experienced temptation (Matt 4:1–11; Luke 4:1–13) and appeared defeated by the power of evil in his death. Most people look to the Synoptics to study the human Jesus, and study the divine Jesus in the Gospel of John. In fact, the Fourth Gospel portrays both the human *and* the divine Jesus.

Logos (Word)

The author used the title *Logos* only in the prologue, although the theology of the "Word of God" dominates the Gospel. John seized upon a term used in both Jewish and Hellenistic circles and used it as his instrument to set forth a part of the Jesus tradition. The theology of the title is broader than its use in the first chapter. Jesus is the Word of God and thus, when he speaks, he reveals God. The words of Jesus, God his father has taught him (John 8:40; 14:10, 24). The content of this word from the Father concerns the person of Jesus and his relationship to the Father and to the disciples. As Word incarnate, he reveals the Father and invites individuals to respond to this revelation.

The prologue itself emphasizes the divinity of Jesus. The Word preexists, functions in creation, gives light and life, reveals the glory of God through the manifestation of grace and truth, returns to the Father from whose side he has never left. The reader can easily picture a divine person with God, descending upon this earth to fulfill a mission, and then returning. The word is divine; Jesus is divine.

The Son of Man

The title *Son of Man* in this Gospel differs significantly from the Synoptics. John emphasizes the preexistence of the Son of Man, as well as his exaltation and glorification. The stress lies on the divine. The author used the title as a characteristic self-designation. The idea in the background seems to be a figure that is archetype of the human race. The Johannine Son of Man descended from heaven and will ascend again.

> No one has ascended into heaven but he who descended from heaven, the Son of Man. (John 3:13)

> Then what if you were to see the Son of Man ascending where he was before? (John 6:62)

Jesus, as Son of Man, continues his union with God and dwells with God. He is the perfect man, the archetype who epitomizes the true and ultimate relationship of individuals with God. His heavenly origin is the basis for his ultimate elevation and glorification as well as his salvific activity. The Father has already set his seal on the Son of Man (John 6:27) and from the Father he has received his transcendent message (John 3:11–13). This becomes the guarantee of his future return (John 6:62). The title carries a sense of preexistence and when people encounter the Son of Man on earth, they face a divine being.

The Son of God

"Son of God" does not appear often in this Gospel. The Gospel was written to help individuals believe that "Jesus is the Christ, the Son of God"...(John 20:31). The title also appears in the opening chapter used by Nathanael, and, in the trial before Pilate (John 19:7). Jesus is the Son of God because God sanctified him and sent him into this world for a mission. Since the title can be used for other divine emissaries, it need not always denote divinity. The close relationship between Jesus and God is better expressed in the use of *Son.*

Jesus as Son

Jesus is God's Son. For John, this expressed the close relationship between Jesus and God. The Son does only what he sees the Father doing:

> ...the Son can do nothing of his own accord, but only what he sees the Father doing; for whatever he does, that the Son does likewise. (John 5:19)

This and similar examples stress the dependence of the Son upon the Father, but other texts also imply equality. The Son, like the Father, gives life (John 5:21); the Son makes people free (John 8:36); the Son gives eternal life (John 3:36; 6:40); and the Father has given judgment to the Son (John 5:22). The Son seems to stand in equality with God and often cannot be completely distinguished from the Father.

The Son Belongs to the Divine World

The Son lives in the divine world and receives all from the Father (John 5:20; 8:47):

> He who comes from above is above all; he who is of the earth belongs to the earth, and of the earth he speaks; he who comes from heaven is above all. He bears witness to what he has seen and heard…. (John 3:31–32)

All that the Son reveals depends on his previous participation in the divine world. The Son came from the divine world and remains always part of this realm.

The Son as Divine Being

For John, a preexistence does not sufficiently explain the Son. He gives to the human Jesus divine prerogatives. As he knows things supernaturally, he also prays differently:

> "Father, I thank thee that thou has heard me. I knew that you hear me always, but I have said this on account of the people standing by…." (John 11:41–42)

Instead of a fear of death, as seen in the Synoptics, Jesus, when facing death, offers a prayer glorifying the divine name (John 12:27–28). As divine, even his captors fall down before him (John 18:6). The title *Son of God* may not signify a divine being, but when *of God* is joined to *Son,* the readers learn the intention of the author to teach belief in a divine being.

The Use of *Ego Eimi* (I Am)

The author used the expression "I am" *(ego eimi)* nine times. Each time, Jesus speaks, addressing a variety of audiences. The exception is found in John 9:9. The blind man responds with the expression *ego eimi* when the bystanders question his identity.

This example differs from all the other times the phrase appears and will help clarify the meaning. In the past some scholars dismissed these sayings as of little consequence. More recently, scholars have viewed the expression as a theophonic formula representing the divine name or presence. Certainly on the lips of the blind man it can mean "I am the one." But the other uses of the expression open up other possibilities.

Source for the Phrase

Several possibilities can explain the origin of the phrase. Some claim it comes from Hellenism; others that it comes from the Jewish tradition, in which *ego eimi* is the Greek translation for the Hebrew expression *'ani hu* found in Deutero-Isaiah, as well as the Jewish practice to substitute *ani* for the Jewish sacred name for God.

The phrase *'ani hu* occurs six times in Isaiah 40–55. The translators of the Hebrew text into Greek (LXX or Septuagint) chose the Greek expression *ego eimi* to translate *'ani hu*. In Isaiah God speaks and uses the phrase to signify the uniqueness of God. It presents God as the Lord of history and creator of the world, closely related to other expressions of divine self-predication, especially the phrase "I am YHWH." In Jewish liturgical practice the words "I" or "He," by themselves, were sometimes used as surrogates for the sacred name. The expression *'ani hu* was used in the liturgy of the feast of Tabernacles and the expression also appears in commentaries on the Passover service.

The Phrase in John

John seems to have selected this terminology to indicate the close relationship between Jesus and God, as well as to indicate that a new age has dawned by his presence:

> I tell you this now, before it takes place, so that when it takes place you may believe that *ego eimi*. (John 13:19)

Jesus answered them:
"I solemnly declare it, before Abraham came to be, *ego eimi*." (John 8:58)

These examples admit of no predicate understood in context. Compare the first with Isaiah 43:10:

"You are my witnesses," says the Lord, "my servants whom I have chosen, to know and believe in me and understand that *I am*. Before me no god was formed and after me there shall be none."

The author of the Gospel underlines the solemnity of the statement by Jesus. Only Jesus could make it, and only those who believe in him could understand its meaning.

The second example helps in the further disclosure of the meaning of the phrase. When the Jews heard *ego eimi,* they took up stones to throw at him (John 8:59). A similar reaction appears in chapter 10:22–39. Jesus is in the Temple and proclaims: "I and the Father are one." The reaction is the same: he has blasphemed and they seek to stone him. The use of *ego eimi* stresses the unity of Father and Son, God and Jesus.

Implied Predicate

Other examples of the use of this phrase admit of a predicate understood. The phrase used in the Garden of Olives raises much interest. The soldiers, with Judas, approach Jesus and his band of disciples. Jesus maintains complete control and asks:

"Who is it you want?" "Jesus the Nazarene," they replied. "I am he," he answered. Now Judas, the one who was to hand him over, was there with them. As Jesus said to them, "I am he," they retreated slightly and fell to the ground. (John 18:5–6)

"I have told you, 'I am he,'" Jesus said. "If I am the one you want, let these men go."(John 18:8)

The translators chose to add the pronoun "he." The Greek phrase is *ego eimi* (I am). From the context the reader can presume that it means "I am the one." But when Jesus said *ego eimi,* they retreated and fell down. In the presence of the divine, the only appropriate reaction is adoration.

Only one example in the Gospel of John finds a parallel in the Synoptics. When Jesus came to his disciples walking on the sea, he announced: "It is I *(ego eimi),* do not be afraid" (Mark 6:50; Matt 14:27). In Deutero-Isaiah *'ani hu* occurs sometimes in association with the power of God over creation, especially his power over the sea. Earlier people often looked upon the sea as an abode of evil spirits, anxious to destroy all who ventured out too far. This may underlie the usage in Mark and Matthew. Perhaps this was the source of the theology used by John in his use of the phrase.

John used the phrase in an absolute sense in verses 8:58 and 13:19. The phrase centers on the divine presence in Jesus. People must recognize the unity between God and Jesus. When Jesus says "Before Abraham came to be, *ego eimi"* (John 8:58), his listeners and readers today should retreat in awe in the presence of the divine.

The Humanity of Jesus

The image of Jesus portrayed in the Fourth Gospel differs significantly from that in the other gospels. Jesus is the eternal Word of God, the heavenly Son of Man, and the Son of God. He alone represents the presence of the eternal God. He appears so divine in outlook that Christians for centuries have used this Gospel to preach the divinity of Jesus and have often overlooked the humanity of Jesus. No one can deny the emphasis on the divinity of Jesus in this Gospel. But to fail to see how this same Jesus is also very human does an injustice to the genius of the Johannine community, its theology, and the individuals responsible for the Gospel. The Gospel of John portrays a human Jesus as well as the divine Jesus.

Although the word existed for all eternity with the Father, no hint at a supernatural origin for Jesus appears in this Gospel.

Matthew and Luke offer the infancy stories about Jesus and both imply that the origin of Jesus was unlike any other human origin: Jesus was virginally conceived. This Gospel, in contrast, refers to Jesus as the son of Joseph:

> We have found the one about whom Moses wrote in the law, and about whom the prophets spoke, I mean Jesus, the son of Joseph, the man from Nazareth. (John 1:45)

> They kept saying, "Is this not Jesus, the son of Joseph, whose father and mother we know?" (John 6:42)

Jesus belongs to a particular family and, unlike Mark who refers to Jesus as the son of Mary (Mark 6:3), John calls him the son of Joseph.

Jesus, His Friends and His Needs

Jesus needed human affection. One of his disciples intimately leans on his breast at the Last Supper; he enjoyed dinner with Martha and Mary and Lazarus (John 12:1–2); he spent time with his mother and brothers and even attended a marriage celebration (John 2:1–11). On his journey to Samaria he grew tired and thirsty. Like thousands before him and after him, he stopped at Jacob's well to rest and to receive refreshment (John 4:6–7). He changed his mind. When the disciples ask him if he intends to go to Jerusalem for the feast of Tabernacles, he declines. Then he changes his mind and goes (John 7:8–10). He does not experience a painful agony in the garden in this Gospel, nor temptation in the desert, but the author preserved some hint at these aspects of his life when he remarks:

> When Jesus saw her weeping, and when he saw the Jews who had come with her weeping, he was deeply moved in spirit so that an involuntary groan burst from him and he trembled with deep emotion. (John 11:33)

Jesus said to them: "Where have you laid him?" "Lord," they said to him, "come and see." Jesus wept...again a groan was wrung from Jesus' inner being. (John 11:34)

"Now my soul is troubled." (John 12:27)

When Jesus had said these things, he was troubled in spirit.... (John 13:21)

The first two examples display the emotion of Jesus as he encounters his friends after the death of Lazarus. The human Jesus sorrows at the death of a friend. The divine Jesus utters a word and Lazarus comes forth. The next examples contain fear and anxiety. He knows he will die but instead of seeking release, he gladly accepts the will of God.

Jesus appears happy in the presence of good friends. He knows bodily needs and experiences sorrow at the death of a friend. He also knows fear and anxiety as he faces death and even experiences the depression of someone betrayed by a friend. Jesus is very human in this Gospel.

Messiah/Christ and Wisdom

Messiah or Christ refers primarily to the humanity of Jesus. The Gospel opens with a confession that Jesus is the Messiah: "We have found the Messiah" (John 1:41). The set purpose of the Gospel in John 20:31 includes belief in Jesus as Messiah. Throughout the Gospel, however, the title implies a spiritual reality rather than a political reality. In several passages in the Old Testament, Wisdom replaces the role of the messiah. In their zeal for the law, some scribes even began to identify the law with Wisdom. Two parallel movements converge on Jesus. A prophetic tradition saw salvation and redemption as God's work through a messiah in history. Wisdom literature depicted salvation and redemption already implanted in creation by God. Individuals who live according to their consciences would discover Wisdom and experience the saving presence of God. The former movement centered on the external; the latter on the internal.

Both concepts are united in the Fourth Gospel. Jesus is incarnate Wisdom. In him people may discover the Wisdom which God has implanted in the universe. Jesus fulfills the law and prophets and is Wisdom incarnate. The title *Christ* focuses on humanity, which expresses divinity. Jesus as the incarnation of Wisdom bears the divine. He cannot be the messiah unless people see a human being who releases all of the possible energies implanted in human nature by a provident God. When the evangelist claims that Jesus is the Messiah, the Christ, he proclaims the human Jesus can lead all to the divine both as fulfilling the prophets and expressing Wisdom.

Conclusion

The Fourth Gospel has long been recognized as emphasizing the divinity of Jesus. The divine Jesus knows everything, never suffers, and fulfills his destiny—always in control. It also preserves his humanity. The author does not, however, resolve the relationship between the two. The Johannine community preserved a particular sensitivity to the divinity of Jesus but would not fall into the mistaken notion that the divinity eclipsed the humanity. With careful progression, the author leads the reader from humanity to divinity without losing anything in the process. The divine Jesus of the Fourth Gospel is the very human Jesus of Nazareth.

The Many Models of Jesus in the New Testament

Even a short overview of the New Testament demonstrates the many images of Jesus, developed from the original experience of the historical Jesus on the part of the early followers of Jesus. He may have been an ordinary Jew from lower Galilee, but he spoke eloquently about the kingdom of God. He had received the baptism of John but had changed the message of John from God as an apocalyptic judge to God who was present in everyday life, offering reconciliation, salvation, and peace. The ecstatic vision of Jesus brought a message of equality for all, patron and peasant, Gentile and Jew, male and female, rich and poor, slave and free. Jesus challenged the Judaism of his time to become inclusive rather than exclusive. Jesus encourages his followers to invite all to table fellowship and forgive all, for God invites all to the fellowship of the table of life and forgives all. So Jesus could be Messiah and Christ for them. He could be Lord and Son of God; he could be friend of all and shepherd of all, healer and miracle worker, prophet and liberator, and above all, savior. People looked upon Jesus and saw the kindness and compassion of God decked out not in majesty, but in the simple apparel of an itinerant preacher. Jesus offered free healing, free fellowship, free grace, free salvation. He offered reconciliation and justification, and a wonderful future for all people and things, begun in the here and now. The Jesus of the New Testament rests upon the faith of many believers in many communities. Reading what others believed of Jesus in the early church helps in understanding Jesus today.

Topics for Discussion

1. John presents Jesus as divine. What value does this image offer?

2. John also presents Jesus as revealing God the Father. How does this help people today?

3. Jesus is very human but more divine in this gospel. Is the author having trouble making up his mind on Jesus?

4. What are your favorite elements in the Jesus of this gospel?

5. Do you find it easier to see Jesus as a friend in this gospel, or do you prefer one of the other gospels?

Works Consulted

Jesus in John

Culpepper, R. Alan, and C. Clifton Black, eds. *Exploring the Gospel of John*. Louisville, KY: Westminster John Knox, 1996.

Karris, Robert. *Jesus and the Marginalized in John's Gospel*. Collegeville, MN: Liturgical Press, 1990.

Matera, Frank. *New Testament Christology*. Louisville, KY: Westminster John Knox, 1999.

O'Grady, John F. *According to John*. New York/Mahwah, NJ: Paulist Press, 1999.

Richard, Earl. *Jesus: One and Many*. Wilmington, DE: Glazier, 1988.

Schnackenburg, Rudolf. *Jesus in the Gospels*. Louisville, KY: Westminster John Knox, 1995.

Chapter Nine

John the Baptist

All four gospels contain narratives about John the Baptist. He appears in each gospel just before Jesus begins his ministry. The New Testament has two forms of his name: John the Baptist as a formal title, and John the Baptizer, emphasizing what he did. Probably the epithet, what he did, historically preceded the title, although most Christians today refer to John as "the Baptist."

Most readers of the gospels know that John lived an ascetical life with a ministry in the Judean desert prior to the advent of Jesus, and he included a ritual washing in his preaching as a sign of repentance. King Herod Antipas killed John probably around 29 CE. The actual historical reason for the execution remains unclear. Perhaps it had something to do with Herodias, the wife of Herod, and Salome, her daughter, or perhaps Herod feared John because of the ever-increasing number of followers, or perhaps some truth is found in both motives.

The relationship between Jesus and John found in the Gospel of Luke seems legendary (Meier: 23ff.). Some history may be found, however, in the Lukan attestation that John came from a priestly family (Brown: 265–66). Josephus, in *Jewish Antiquities*, refers to John as a good man who had urged the Jews to lead a righteous life, but whom Herod had put to death. Josephus believes that the death sentence came from a suspicious Herod who feared John. He makes no mention of any relationship to Herodias and Salome. Later, Josephus remarks that the defeat of Herod's armies by Aretas King of Petra was a divine vindication of John (Meier: 56–62).

Some will try to relate John to the Essene community at Qumran near the Dead Sea. No definite evidence supports this theory, but it cannot be categorically denied (Meier: 25–26). Some also think that Jesus was once part of this Jewish monastic community. Again, both remain theories without solid historical evidence.

John the Prophet

No doubt exists, however, that John lived apart from society. Many might regard him as alienated from his society and culture. He lives in the desert and clothes himself in camel's hair, eating locusts and wild honey (Mark 1:6). Not only his way of living but also his actual preaching attacked the ordinary elements of his society. He denounced the injustice of the Jerusalem elite and criticized all for their lack of piety. They all needed to change their way of living. If indeed he was part of a priestly family, he would have been expected to follow the vocation of his father. Instead he seems to have abandoned any possibility of marriage and raising a son to continue the lineage of priesthood, turning his back on priestly duty in the Temple and embracing a prophetic vocation in the wilderness, announcing the judgment of God.

Like the prophets of old, John separated himself from the conventions of society. He found the contemporary way of living to be wanting. The Essenes were probably a group of lower level priests, alienated from the clergy of Jerusalem, who wished to live a simpler life based on the Torah and avoid all ostentation. Whether John was part of this community or not, he and the Essenes shared similar beliefs (Meier: 25). Both separated themselves from Jerusalem and from the higher clergy in the holy city.

Both also engaged in ascetical practices. Both the Essenes and John preached a radical return to Jewish traditions.

Josephus and the Dead Sea Scrolls support the opinion that a great gulf separated the aristocratic clergy in Jerusalem from the lower clergy in the rural areas (Hollenbach: 892). It seems that some of these aristocratic religious leaders came and listened to John. Their motivation, however, remains unknown. Perhaps some came to spy on him, and perhaps some came with sincerity. Maybe others came to scoff, but left repentant. In all likelihood John did affect some of the nobility, but probably not too many. His ministry, like that of Jesus, would be accepted more by the poor and lowly than by the high and mighty.

The Ministry of John for Jesus

The ministry of John and Jesus may have overlapped, and they may have died within a year of each other. Three of the four gospels record the baptism of Jesus by John, although each has its own interpretation on what happened. In Luke, for example, it is not clear who baptized Jesus since John was already in prison.

> ...for all the evil things Herod had done, added this to them all, that he shut up John in prison. Now when all the people were baptized, and when Jesus also had been baptized and was praying.... (Luke 3:19–21)

The Fourth Gospel alone does not record the baptism of Jesus but alludes to it (Jonn 1:29–34). Historically, John probably baptized Jesus. He also separates his baptism from one that will come after him. He baptizes in water but this second baptism will be by fire and the Spirit (Matt 3:11; Luke 3:16). John clearly depreciates his own baptism in favor of one that will come. Christians recognize the second baptism as the one coming from Jesus which will be a purifying baptism of the Spirit. Repentant sinners will receive this final purifying baptism while those who refuse to repent will experience the judgment of God. Those who do repent must express this new way of living in how they act. The ritual washing demands a change in living.

Ritual Washings

The ancient world knew many forms of ritual washing. The Old Testament prescribes such washings (Lev 14:5–6, 50–52; Num 19:13, 20–21; Isa 1:16) which some Jews carry out to this day. Even ritual washings in the wilderness were not uncommon, including rituals at Qumran (Meier: 50). Unlike Qumran, however, John seems to have administered his baptism only once to his followers, emphasizing its eschatological and final character. Mark adds that the baptism was a baptism of repentance for the remission of sins (Mark 1:4). But this phrase appears only in Mark and in the Lucan parallel (Luke 3:3) dependent upon Mark. Matthew has the phrase, but instead of relating it to baptism he joins it to the Eucharist (Matt 3:1–2, 11, compare to 26:28). Like the Christian understanding of sacraments, the baptism of John expressed a reality already present: the desire to change a way of living, experience a forgiveness of sins, avoid divine judgment, and ultimately experience the outpouring of the Spirit of God. The ritual meant nothing unless the persons changed their way of living. Even for Jesus, his baptism brought about a change in living for he began his public ministry after his baptism.

Unanswered Questions

Certain questions remain: Who were the original audience of John? Was he the prophet who gave a message to all the people or did he first concentrate on a small group? Who are the brood of vipers? Did John expect an overthrow of the social order? Did he preach in Jerusalem? Many think that John directed his message first to the powerful of Jerusalem. He wanted them to change their way of living and dealing with people. Then perhaps others came out to listen to John (Hollenbach: 893–95). When John speaks of the "brood of vipers," some think he refers specifically to the high-living aristocrats, especially those of the priestly caste. A change by the aristocrats would surely imply a change in the social order. Recent archaeological work has discovered a high level of luxury in Jerusalem around the Temple area. Like the prophets of old, John denounced the oppression of the poor and the luxury of the wealthy. But John must have begun preaching to a small group before reaching the larger group. Like Jesus, he may have thought people, especially religious and civil leaders, would pay attention. In the end he appealed more to the poor and lowly, as did Jesus.

The gospels narrate that John verbally attacked Herod Antipas for his way of living (Mark 6:17–18; Luke 3:19). If he wished Herod to repent he surely expected those around Herod to change their way of living. They should all do works of repentance (Matt 3:8) and social justice (Luke 3:10–14). He used a ritual washing in the Jordan for a sign of this repentance. Just as water cleanses, so the baptism of John would give new life to the repentant ones. When he actually baptized, the gospels claim that he also joined his washing to teaching about the one that would come (Luke 3:16–17). Whether this was the historical John anticipating the baptism promulgated by Jesus or that of the followers of Jesus claiming the superiority of the baptism of Jesus, remains another unanswered question. No one can be sure if John proclaimed the coming of the Messiah and the reign of God in Jesus. He clearly, however, followed the tradition of the Old Testament prophets who called for social justice or else experience the judgment of God.

Of course, reading the gospels raises still another question: Where did John preach? If he preached in the desert or wilderness, how did people learn about him? By word of mouth? Is the desert and wilderness near the Jordan River—for the actual baptism? If he wanted the leaders to reform, would they go to the desert to see some ascetic? Probably John initially preached in towns and marketplaces, and then perhaps he met people in less populated areas to continue his instruction. If Herod was suspicious, probably

John also preached in Jerusalem. This fits in well with the gospel story of Herodias and Salome. Just as Jesus fulfilled his ministry as an itinerant preacher, so the same was true for John. He preached hope for those who repented and judgment for those of bad faith, probably all over Israel and Judah.

John in Mark

In the first written Gospel, Mark, John arrives on the scene, preaches a gospel of repentance, is handed over and dies (Mark 1:4, 14). In this same Gospel, Jesus experiences the same treatment. Jesus arrives on the scene, preaches, is handed over and dies (Mark 1:14–15; 9:31). The same is true for the disciples of Jesus (Mark 3:14; 13:9). John proclaimed that someone mightier would come after him, offering a baptism in the Holy Spirit (Mark 1:7–8). But as noted, whether this was part of the original preaching of John or added by Christians remains unknown. John gathered disciples who joined him in prayer and fasting (Mark 2:18), and some of them buried him when he was murdered (Mark 6:29). He also baptized Jesus (Mark 1:9). Herod arrested John and killed him because John criticized Herod for marrying his brother's wife, at the instigation of Herodias (Mark 6:17–19). John was present at the beginning of the ministry of Jesus and then fades from the scene.

John in Matthew

The author of the second written Gospel accepts some of the traditions from Mark and adds to them concerning John. His preaching is not only to issue calls for repentance, but also to announce that the kingdom of God is at hand (Matt 3:2). Jesus preaches the same message (Matt 4:17). Mark implied that John was Elijah, the forerunner of the Messiah, but Matthew makes it explicit (Matt 3:3). Both John and Jesus call for the righteous to believe the message. Those who are not righteous (both for Jesus and John)—the Pharisees, Herod, and other religious leaders—refuse to believe and they decide to kill them both. Matthew concludes with the comment that as great as John was, the least in the kingdom of God is greater (Matt 11:9–14).

John in Luke

Most commentators today think that the Lucan story of John and his family was created by the author using Old Testament sources (Meier: 23–27). He fits into history, but Luke's understanding of history. Jesus himself presents Luke's perspective in his comment: "The law and the prophets were until John; since then the good news of the kingdom of God is preached" (Luke 16:16). John fits into Luke's historical scheme: Law and prophets (including John) first, and then Jesus and the Christian Church (Conzelmann). What especially characterizes John in Luke is the parallel to Jesus regarding the announcement of their births, their mothers' relationship, their actual births, and the superiority of Jesus over John (Brown: 248–50). The same continues in the references to John in the Acts of the Apostles (1:5; 13:24; 19:3–6). Luke presents John as a transitional figure between the Old Testament and Jesus. John finishes the Old Testament and Jesus begins the New. Also in Luke, Jesus remarks that the ordinary people, including sinners, accepted the baptism of John, while the Pharisees and scribes rejected what God was offering them in John (Luke 7:29–30).

John in the Fourth Gospel

Unlike the other gospels, the author of this final Gospel never refers to John as the Baptist or the Baptizer, and does not record John baptizing Jesus. In this Gospel John exists as a witness and nothing more. He is a man sent from God whose name was John (John 1:6). Even the fact of John baptizing is not introduced until verse 25. The John of this Gospel is the John of Christian faith

(Collins: 33). He comes to give testimony, to bear witness to the light (John 1:7). Even the first Johannine narrative begins with "And this is the testimony of John" (John 1:19). As a believer, John confesses that Jesus is the Lamb of God (John 1:29) and the one on whom the Spirit descends and remains (John 1:32). Finally, he testifies that: "I have seen and have borne witness that this is the Son of God" (John 1:34). The final remark of Jesus about John expresses the attitude of the author of the Fourth Gospel:

> You sent to John, and he has borne witness to the truth.
> Not that the testimony which I receive is from man; but
> I say this that you may be saved. He was a burning and
> shining lamp, and you were willing to rejoice for a while
> in his light. (John 5:33–35)

The bright and shining light shone on Jesus as the one sent from God to bring life and light. He pointed out Jesus on whom the Spirit of God descended and remained. John fulfilled his destiny by offering testimony about Jesus to all who would listen. Then John faded from the scene.

John and Historical Turmoil

Like the prophets already studied, Isaiah and Jeremiah, John the Baptist can be understood only within the context of his moment in history along with the perennial commitment to the religious traditions of Israel. As true in most periods of human history, those in power and with wealth use and abuse those who have neither. This becomes particularly difficult to accept when these same people lay claim to some religious foundation for their lives and actions. In times of crises these situations become more acute. Varieties of social and religious turmoil result. Such was the condition following the death of Herod the Great in 4 BCE, the rule of Pontius Pilate from 26–36 CE, and just before the Jewish wars in 66–70 CE, culminating in the destruction of the Temple by Titus in 70 CE. Into this period fall both John and Jesus.

John and His Ministry

As far back as David, the priests in Jerusalem looked down on the rural priests of the tribes living outside of the city. Such was probably the case at the time of John. Accepting the historical good possibility that John came from a priestly family, he would have been disturbed by the treatment by the aristocratic clergy of Jerusalem and repulsed by the contrast with their lifestyle, and that of both clergy and people in the rural areas. Calling first to the leaders to repent by returning to the desert traditions of the people of Israel, he would have turned more and more to the ordinary people to offer them hope. To the unrepentant, John called upon the wrath of God to destroy them and their way of life. Alienated from his society, the personality of John drove him to a simpler and ascetical life not unlike the Christian desert fathers in the early years of Christianity. As has happened often in history, those with power and wealth responded negatively and contributed to the demise of John. For those who responded positively, he promised a better future that early Christian writers interpreted as the following of Jesus. Initiating the example of John, his followers practiced a more just social order. To support their vision, the followers of John also adapted his practice of fasting and prayer. Like the prophets of the Old Testament, John suffered and died for telling the truth.

John knew his calling. He announced another and not himself. He willingly decreased as Jesus increased. He never pretended to be someone other than who he was. He told the truth to leaders, both civil and religious, and never shrank from his vocation to point out the presence and absence of God to the people of his times. Telling the truth caused trouble for John but the problems and suffering did not stop him. Ultimately his love of truth led him to a martyr's death. John knew who he was, accepted his call, spoke the truth, never pretended to be anyone else, announced another's coming, and died. The effort to give light to others consumed the "bright and shining light," John the Baptist.

Topics for Discussion

1. How is John like the prophets of the Old Testament?

2. Why are some people upset about lifestyles, especially of religious leaders?

3. What virtues of John impress you?

4. Does suffering always come to those who tell the truth?

5. How would you like to imitate John the Baptist?

6. Why are John and Jesus so similar?

7. Do you like people who announce themselves? Explain.

8. Why was John a "bright and shining light"?

Works Consulted

Brown, Raymond. *The Birth of the Messiah*. New York: Doubleday, 1993.

Collins, Raymond. "The Representative Figures of the Fourth Gospel." *Downside Review* 91 (1976): 26–46, 118–32.

Conzelmann, Hans. *The Theology of Saint Luke*. London: Faber and Faber, 1961.

Hollenbach, Paul W. "John the Baptist," *The Anchor Bible Dictionary*. New York: Doubleday, 1993, 887–99.

Meier, John. *A Marginal Jew*, vol. II. New York: Doubleday, 1994.

PART IV

Followers of Jesus

Jesus had numerous followers, both men and women. Some mentioned in the New Testament actually knew Jesus in his ministry, while others, especially Paul, had no contact with Jesus while he lived in Israel. Paul claimed to have had a personal revelation of Jesus. Others preached and wrote about him with no effort to lay claim to such an experience.

Certainly the twelve apostles/disciples might claim to have known Jesus best, but modern scholarship believes that not one of the Twelve ever wrote about Jesus. The Gospel of Matthew is ascribed to one of the Twelve as is the Gospel of John, but in all probability, all of the gospels are from anonymous authors.

Peter has two letters ascribed to him, but they were probably written long after Peter had been martyred. People can learn about Peter from the four gospels and each gospel has its own portrait.

Paul wrote many letters, some of which are surely lost while others have been preserved and have become part of the New Testament. In the New Testament, some letters are also ascribed to Paul which he did not write. The Acts of the Apostles tell stories about both Peter and Paul, but in recent scholarship many of the historical details of the Acts has been questioned. How much history and how much embroidered history decorates the lives of these earliest followers of Jesus may never be known.

Probably the Christian Church knows more about Paul than any other follower. The New Testament has his genuine letters. The contemporary followers of Jesus may also know more about the Beloved Disciple, at least about his personality, even if we do not know his name.

Judas has always been an enigma for Christians. Jesus offered so much and yet he seems to have been oblivious of the meaning of Jesus. In honesty, however, did any one of the Twelve grasp what Jesus meant by his teachings?

Like any story, those associated with the earliest followers of Jesus have developed in the telling. Peter is always the spokesperson of the Twelve, but clearly inferior to the Beloved Disciple in the Fourth Gospel. Luke depicts Paul as the apostle devoted to the church, with no controversy with church leaders. Paul himself acknowledges his problems with the "pillars of the church" (Gal 2:9). Much depends on why the authors wrote about the particular individuals.

Like the personalities in the Old Testament, these men have both virtues and vices, with the possible exception of the Beloved Disciple. Like the mother of Jesus in the Fourth Gospel this follower of Jesus lives as the model of the perfect male follower of Jesus. He had no vices.

Perhaps at different times in life, individuals will identify with different followers of the Lord. These individuals, like those of the Old Testament, will also function in the same manner as the story of Adam and Eve or the parables of Jesus. Looking at Peter, Paul, the Beloved Disciple, and Judas acts like a window to view life. Then they become mirrors reflecting the self with the hope that the personalities will again become a window and the person looking will see life differently.

Chapter Ten

Peter

Roman Catholics probably think more often of Peter than do other Christians. For Catholics, Peter functioned as the first bishop of Rome and the first pope. The present Holy Father continues the long tradition, tracing his lineage back to Peter, and the pope claims the Vicar of Peter as one of his titles (an older title than the Vicar of Christ). Most Christians who read the Bible often, however, also may think that they know more about Peter than any other of the twelve apostles, since he appears more frequently in the New Testament than any other of the Twelve. Most Christians also tend to like Peter. They can identify with him. Bold and tempestuous, Peter betrayed Jesus in his moment of need. But in spite of his many failings (Herron: 142–44), Peter lived and died as a person of faith. Such a person can encourage individual believers today as they too struggle with living a life of faith.

The New Testament makes many references to Peter. In each gospel, Jesus calls Peter and his brother Andrew to be his disciples (Mark 1:16–20; Matt 4:18–22; Luke 5:1–11 [Luke omits Andrew]). The Gospel of John presents Andrew as a follower of John the Baptizer, and he calls his brother Peter to come and meet Jesus (John 1:40–42). Jesus heals the mother-in-law of Peter, recorded in three gospels (Mark 1:29–31; Matt 8:14–15; Luke

4:38–39). Peter along with Andrew and John also witnesses the healing of the daughter of Jarius (Mark 5:37), the Transfiguration (Mark 9:2; Matt 17:1; Luke 9:28), and the agony in the garden (Mark 14:33; Matt 26:37). At the Last Supper, Peter boasts that he will remain faithful to Jesus even to death (Mark 14:29–31; Matt 26:33–35; Luke 22:31–34; John 13:36–38). While the other members of the Twelve flee after the arrest of Jesus, Peter follows Jesus into the courtyard of the high priest only to deny Jesus (Mark 14:54, 66–72; Matt 26:58, 69–75; Luke 22:54–62; John 18:15–27). Peter tries to walk on the water but fails (Matt 14:28). He attempts to use violence in the garden (John 18:10–11), but Jesus does not allow it. Peter often acts without thinking and always struggles with faith. No wonder he appeals to many.

Professions of Faith

In addition to these appearances, Peter also makes four confessions of faith. In Mark 8:27b–29, Jesus asks:

> "Who do men say that I am?" And they told him, "John the Baptist; and others say Elijah; and others one of the prophets." And he asked them, "But who do you say that I am?" Peter answered him, "You are the Christ."

In the parallel place in Matthew, Peter adds: "You are the Christ, the Son of the living God" (Matt 16:16). And according to Luke, Peter answered, "The Christ of God" (Luke 9:20). In the Gospel of John, Peter has a fuller response:

> Simon Peter answered him, "Lord, to whom shall we go? You have the words of eternal life; and we have believed, and have come to know that you are the Holy One of God." (John 6:68–69)

The early church evidently never lost sight of Peter's commitment to Jesus, even if he did not always act as a person of faith.

Stories about Peter

The gospels also contain many stories and anecdotes about Peter, and each one allows further understanding of his character. In Matthew 14:25–31, as noted, Peter attempts to walk on the water. The disciples had been out fishing on rough seas and are frightened when they see Jesus coming toward them. Peter yells, "If it is you, Lord, command me to come to you on the water." Jesus says, "Come," and Peter ventured out on the water, only to find himself sinking and he had to call to the Lord to save him. In the Gospel of John, Peter jumps into the water from the boat when they are only a hundred yards off shore because he wants to be with Jesus (John 21:7–8). He seems to act before he thinks.

At the transfiguration, while Peter and James remain silent, Peter blurts out: "Master, it is well that we are here; let us make three booths, one for you and one for Moses and one for Elijah" (Mark 9:5; Matt 17:4; Luke 9:33). Evidently Peter neither understood nor was smart enough to remain quiet. Often he speaks before thinking. His profession of faith in John 6:67 may be a quick retort ("Where shall we go?"), with a quick addition: "You have the words of eternal life." In chapter 21 of the Fourth Gospel, his remark about the Beloved Disciple—"What about this man?" (John 21:21)—may also contain a certain disdain. Peter says what comes to his mind.

Pious Peter recognizes his own sinfulness and the holiness of Jesus. After fishing all night without a catch, and after Jesus instructs them to put down their nets and they load up two boats, Peter remarks: "Depart from me, for I am a sinful man, O Lord" (Luke 5:8). The same pious Peter wants to defend himself concerning forgiveness and asks Jesus how many times he must forgive (Matt 18:21–22). Generous as he is, Peter is willing to forgive up to seven times. He must have been disappointed when Jesus said "seventy times seven." Finally, pious Peter does not wish Jesus to wash his feet at the Last Supper (John 13:6–10), but when Jesus tells him he cannot share in his inheritance unless Jesus washes his feet, Peter impetuously asks Jesus to wash his hands and his head as well.

The Failure and the Forgiven

Both in Mark 8:32–33 and Matthew 16:21–23, Jesus calls Peter "Satan," the tempter. In Matthew, Jesus also calls Peter an obstacle, a *skandalon*. Peter does not wish Jesus to talk about pain and suffering and so acts as a temptation and an obstacle to Jesus. Peter seems interested in glory and honor—anything but pain and suffering. Jesus rejects Peter's understanding of ministry. In reality, Peter will suffer the same fate as his master:

> "Truly, truly, I say to you, when you were young, you girded yourself and walked where you would; but when you are old, you will stretch out your hands and another will gird you and carry you where you do not wish to go." (This he said to show by what death he was to glorify God.) (John 21:18–19)

The over-confident Peter proclaimed that he would remain faithful even if all others would abandon Jesus (Matt 26:31–35), and proceeded to do just that. And as noted, when surrounded by soldiers the same over-confident Peter drew his sword and cut off the high priest's servant's ear (John 18:10; Luke 22:50; Mark 14:47; Matt 26:51). John alone says it was Peter who struck the servant. Peter thought he knew everything and how everything should work out, and he not only spoke but acted. Finally, Peter experiences forgiveness and rehabilitation in the final chapter of the Gospel of John. Three times Jesus asks Peter if he loves him and three times Peter replies yes (John 21:15–17). In the final Gospel, with Peter's expression of faith in jumping into the water to go to Jesus on the shore, and his commitment to love Jesus, Peter receives a pastoral ministry in the church. Each gospel presents different aspects of the personality and history of Peter. All the gospels agree, however, that he functioned as a leader, but each gospel has its own approach to Peter (Perkins).

Peter the Leader

Peter as head of the apostolic group, and the role of Peter in the New Testament and the early church, have produced numerous studies (R. Brown, K. Donfried, and J. Reumann) which affect contemporary Christianity. In the ministry of Jesus, Peter was one of the earliest called to follow the Lord, but not necessarily the first. He was prominent among the Twelve, as evidenced by his name being placed first in the listing of the apostles (Mark 3:15; Matt 10:2). But Simon Peter did not function in solitary splendor, for in the gospel stories he is frequently associated with other prominent disciples, for example James and John and sometimes Andrew in the Synoptic tradition, and with the Beloved Disciple in the Johannine tradition. Peter is important but never isolated from the others. Each gospel presents his role and joins him with other followers of Jesus.

Peter in Mark and Matthew

Peter made a confession of faith in the Lord (Mark 8:30; Matt 16:6; Luke 9:20; John 6:69) during the ministry of Jesus, but readers are unable to evaluate this confession of faith completely since a critical analysis of the Gospel of Mark, the first written Gospel, seems to indicate that Jesus did not accept this confession by Peter. Matthew, on the contrary, has Jesus praise Peter for his profession of faith:

> Simon Peter replied, "You are the Christ, the Son of the living God." And Jesus answered him, "Blessed are you, Simon Bar-Jona! For flesh and blood has not revealed this to you, but my Father who is in heaven. And I tell you, you are Peter, and upon this rock I will build my church, and the powers of death shall not prevail

against it. I will give you the keys of the kingdom of
heaven, and whatever you bind on earth shall be bound
in heaven, and whatever you loose on earth shall be
loosed in heaven."(Matt 16:16–19)

In the profession of faith by Peter in Mark and Luke, the
long section on Peter as head of the church is missing. In
Matthew, Peter shares in the ministry of Jesus, but Matthew does
not settle the exact nature of this authority. Although he singles
Peter out for special blessing from God that enables Peter to recognize Jesus as the Son of the living God, Matthew does not distin-
guish his authority, for in chapter 18 the other disciples also
have the authority to bind and loose (Matt 18:18). Matthew also
notes Peter's weakness, for in this same chapter in verse 23 Jesus
rebukes Peter and calls him a stumbling block, a *skandalon.* He
who would be the rock upon which the church would be built is
also a stumbling block to the Lord (Stock). The authority of
Peter in the Gospel of Matthew is evident in the choice of the
word *keys,* but whether this is qualitatively different from the
authority given to the others in this same Gospel remains moot.
Also, whether the saying is taken from a post-resurrection
appearance of Jesus and projected back into the ministry of the
Lord remains another unanswered question. Peter appears prominent in this Gospel, and for this reason Matthew was used more
frequently in a Roman Catholic tradition that stressed the apostolic continuity between Peter and the bishops of Rome. The
author of this Gospel also presents Peter as an example of a cen-
trist approach to Christianity (O'Grady, 1989: 155–56). But it
should also be noted that the context in which Peter is given his
authority is his recognition of Jesus as the Son of the living God.
The authority of Peter is related to his faith in Jesus (Brown:
83–101). Jesus gives Peter in the Gospel of Matthew a central
role in the church. Peter may be weak but his weakness does not
deny him his position in early Christianity. Matthew makes sure
of that.

Peter in Luke and in the Acts of the Apostles

Several passages in Luke's Gospel are parallel to Mark and Matthew, but one passage during the Last Supper presents another image of Peter proper to Luke. Following the institution of the Eucharist, he describes a dispute among the apostles (Luke 22:14) as to who will be the greatest. Jesus responds with a parabolic statement concerning the obligation of the leader to serve, and promises the apostles a place of honor because they have continued with him in his trials. Luke offers his prediction of the fall of Peter in a different context than Mark and Matthew, for here the apostles are faithful in the trials (Luke 22:28). Their falling away is obliquely hinted at in verse 32, which forms the context of the prediction of the denial of Peter and his mission to strengthen his brothers:

> "Simon, Simon, behold, Satan demanded you to sift like wheat but I have prayed for you that your faith may not fail. And when you have turned again, strengthen your brothers." (Luke 22:31–32)

The meaning of brothers here has a wider understanding than the apostles, and the strengthening refers to his post-resurrection role as described in the Acts when Peter takes on his missionary role as the leading spokesman for the faith of the Jerusalem community. Peter will be the most active apostle in the Acts of the Apostles, and in that work he is given a role as a leader of the community. The role of Peter as strengthening his brothers is connected to faith. Jesus has prayed for Peter and thus Peter cannot lay personal claim to faith. As in Matthew, the faith of Peter is a gift from the Father in heaven. In Luke, Peter's role of strengthening involves a hortatory or missionary function, while the role that Matthew gives Peter as rock has the function of a foundation. The former implies a continual activity while the latter is a once-and-for-all function. The strengthening aspect of the role of Peter in Luke is parallel to the role given to Peter in the Fourth Gospel.

Frequently in the Acts of the Apostles Peter figures prominently. Following the gospels, Peter's name appears first among the
apostles (Acts 1:13) and he guides the election of Matthias (Acts
1:15–26). Peter preaches in Jerusalem and outside Jerusalem. (Acts
2:14–26; 3:12–26; 4:8–12; 5:29–32; 10:34–43). Peter works miracles (Acts 3:1–10; 5:1–11, 15; 9:32–42). He remains an object of
divine care and receives a vision (Acts 5: 17–21; 10:9–48;
12:6–11) and functions as the spokesperson for the community
(Acts 2:14–36; 8:14–25; 11:1–18). Acts demonstrates that Peter's
ministry extended beyond Jerusalem. He was not a local church
leader but involved with the universal church. This is demonstrated in the discussion with Paul in Jerusalem in Acts 15. After
this episode, Peter is not again mentioned in the Acts of the
Apostles (Donfried: 253–54). Like Matthew, Luke presents Peter
as a significant follower of Jesus during the ministry of Jesus and a
leader in the development of the early church.

Peter in the Fourth Gospel

Throughout the Fourth Gospel, the author places Peter and
the Beloved Disciple in contrast. If the Beloved Disciple was not
one of the Twelve, but still an eyewitness and disciple of the Lord,
this can explain why he would not emphasize the role of the
Twelve (Schnackenburg: 375–88). If the Beloved Disciple also
maintained a pastoral ministry not based on the authority of the
Twelve, he would be contrasted with the leader of the Twelve. In
the epilogue of the Gospel, however, the author gives to Peter a
share in the pastoral ministry of Jesus. The threefold question:
"Simon, son of John, do you love me?" (John 21:15–17) reflects
Peter's threefold denial and thus the scene is often referred to as the
rehabilitation of Peter. The imagery is pastoral, implying an eccle-
sial role for Peter. The shepherd feeds his sheep, leads them to pas-
ture, and protects them. Following the same imagery in chapter 10
of this Gospel, the shepherd enjoys an intimacy with the sheep: he
knows them by name and they recognize his voice. Finally, follow-

ing the example of the good shepherd parable, Peter the new shepherd will lay down his life for his sheep. The command to feed the sheep implies a pastoral ministry over the sheep, but the context for this share in the ministry of Jesus should not be forgotten: Peter must love Jesus and be willing to die for the sheep. At this period of the early church, some individuals exercised authority over the members of the community and no doubt some traced their authority to Peter (O'Grady, 1979: 62). By recalling the context of this authority, the author of the Gospel of John specifies on what this ministry will depend: the love of the Lord and the willingness to die for the sheep. The imagery of authority is stronger in Matthew than in John but in John it is stronger than in Luke. The remark in 1 Peter 5:1–4 attributed to Peter speaking to his fellow presbyters also fits into this context of ministry:

> Tend the flock of God that is in your charge exercising oversight *(episkopein)* not by constraint but willingly ...not as domineering over those in your charge but being examples to the flock. And when the chief Shepherd is manifested, you will obtain the unfading crown of glory. (1 Peter 5:2–4)

Presbyters such as Peter will have the example of the good shepherd as the model for their ministry. The context of this share in the ministry of Jesus founds the ministry of Peter: a love of Jesus and a willingness to die for the sheep. For anyone to share in the pastoral ministry of Jesus, he must be willing to follow the example of the good shepherd. (John 21:18–19). The final editor of this Gospel would accept the authority of Peter and his successors but would remind those who shared in this authority of the conditions for its exercise.

Peter in the Writings of Paul

Paul refers to Peter and Cephas in Galatians (1:18; 2:7–11, 14) and in 1 Corinthians (1:12; 3:22; 9:5; 15:5) refers to Cephas alone without the addition of Peter. The most positive reference is the last one in which Paul notes that the risen Lord appeared to Cephas and then to the Twelve. In Galatians, Paul acknowledges that Peter is a leader of the church in Jerusalem and that he has an apostolate to the Jews. Paul has his problems with Cephas/Peter mainly because he originally shared fellowship with Gentile Christians, but then when confronted by some Jewish Christians, Peter withdrew that fellowship, fearing the Jews (Gal 2:11–14). At a time of extreme Jewish nationalism, Jews would have been very critical of anyone who placed Gentiles in the same position with God as Jews. Perhaps Peter decided to avoid further problems and confrontation but compared to Paul, Peter seems weak and Paul confronts him.

Paul clearly accepts Peter as the first to whom the risen Christ appeared. He also was the source of the tradition about Jesus, acted as leader in the Jerusalem church, and had a ministry to the circumcised. Paul accepted Peter, but also maintained his own right to fulfill an apostolate not inferior to Peter's. The two apostles may not have gotten along too well but each seemed to have recognized the ministry of the other (Donfried: 251–53). Paul had his authority and Peter had his. Provided they preached he same gospel, Paul willingly accepted the authority of Peter.

Conclusion: Peter the Saint and Sinner

Peter began his career as a fisherman, and from the remarks in John 21, he continued to fish after the crucifixion and resurrection of Jesus. He eventually fished for people and died a martyr's death in Rome. Bold and impetuous, he spoke before he thought; he liked to wear a mantle of the pious follower; he wanted Jesus to live gloriously without any suffering; and he had a penchant for jumping into the lake. The first time he almost drowned; the last time he put his clothes on before he jumped and could have rowed to shore faster than swimming. Brash and overconfident, he betrayed Jesus, seemingly without much concern.

Peter the saint believed in Jesus and loved Jesus. He led the smaller band of the Twelve; the somewhat larger group of apostles, including Paul; and finally, all the disciples. Peter preached and healed and traveled throughout the Roman world. Continuing the ministry of Jesus, legend has him dying crucified upside down, for by that time he considered himself unworthy to die in the manner his Master had died. Good and bad, weak and strong, bold and timid, courageous and fearful, sinner and saint. Peter was them all. The faith of Peter saved him as did the faith of Paul and everyone else. The weak apostle became the rock of the church because of that same faith. No one has to be perfect to be a follower of Jesus.

Topics for Discussion

1. Why does Peter appeal to many people?

2. Was Peter a rock or a marshmallow?

3. Why is the faith of Peter so important?

4. Do you think Peter liked the Beloved Disciple?

5. What are some of the many images of Peter in the New Testament?

6. Is piety a detriment to human development?

7. How can vices and virtues exist side by side in people?

Works Consulted

Brown, R., K. Donfried, and J. Reumann. *Peter in the New Testament*. New York: Paulist Press, 1973.

Donfried, Karl. "Peter," *The Anchor Bible Dictionary*, vol. 5. New York: Doubleday, 1992, 251–63.

Herron, Robert W. *Peter's Denial of Jesus: A History of Its Interpretation*. New York: University Press of America, 1991.

O'Grady, John F. *The Four Gospels and the Jesus Tradition.* New York/Mahwah, NJ: Paulist Press, 1989.

———. "The Role of the Beloved Disciple." *Biblical Theology Bulletin* 9 (1979): 58–65.

Perkins, Pheme. *Peter.* Minneapolis: Fortress, 2000.

Schnackenburg, Rudolf. *The Gospel According to St. John,* vol. 3. New York: Crossroad, 1975.

Stock, Augustine. "Is Matthew's Presentation of Peter Ironic?" *Biblical Theology Bulletin* 17 (1987): 64–69.

Chapter Eleven

The Beloved Disciple

Depending on how one counts, the Beloved Disciple appears from five to nine times in the Fourth Gospel. Five times the author explicitly refers to the Beloved Disciple (John 13:23–26; 19:25–27; 20:2–10; 21:7, 20). On two occasions in the final chapter 21, verses 23 and 24, the author used just the word *disciple* with the demonstrative pronoun *this,* seemingly referring to the Beloved Disciple. Some will attempt to identify him as well with the unknown disciple in chapter 1:35. Most will also identify him with the unknown disciple in 18:15. But who is this unnamed disciple? Nowhere is the name *John* ever mentioned, and yet from the second to the twentieth century, most Christians have concluded that the Beloved Disciple was John, the Son of Zebedee, one of the twelve apostles. As recent as some thirty years ago within the Roman Catholic tradition, Raymond Brown in his commentary (1966: C[p.100]), and Rudolf Schnackenburg in his first volume of his commentary (1968: 85), but not his third volume, identified the author in this traditional manner. In his third volume Schnackenburg, in an appendix, writes of the Beloved Disciple as not one of the Twelve, and probably a follower of Jesus from Jerusalem (1982: 375–88). Brown, in his now well-established *The Community of the Beloved Disciple,* joins Schnackenburg in separating the author from the twelve apostles, and of course he is not John the

Son of Zebedee (1979: 31–34). Neither Brown nor Schnacken-burg, nor most other contemporary commentators, seek to identify this unknown author. He is just one of the unnamed disciples in chapter 21:2.

Possible Candidates

Some, however, still follow the quest and seek to identify this unknown author. In 1992, Joseph Grassi in his *The Secret Identity of the Beloved Disciple* studied five candidates as the possible author of the Fourth Gospel: John the Son of Zebedee, Lazarus, John Mark, John the Presbyter, or perhaps the Beloved Disciple as not a historical figure but a literary type. In that same year the German exegete W. Schmithals added to the list of Grassi: the rich young ruler, a beloved brother of Jesus, the unknown disciple of Mark 14:51–52, Andrew, and Nathanael. James Charlesworth not only offers a thorough study of all of the above possibilities but also offers his own opinion that the Beloved Disciple was Thomas, one of the Twelve. A. Culpepper examined ten possibilities, adding to the above: Matthias, Paul, and Benjamin. He also adds that perhaps the Beloved Disciple symbolizes Gentile Christianity, or an itinerant and prophetic community, or the author of the epistles. In fact, over the years more than twenty possibilities have been offered.

Does it make any difference? Does the identity of the Beloved Disciple contribute to the understanding of the Gospel and the contemporary believer, or is this just another exercise for scholars to use to fill up pages of periodicals and books? Can and should any Christian identify with this unknown disciple? Should all Christians identify with him? Is the character of the Beloved Disciple more important than his historicity?

No one can definitively identify the author of the Fourth Gospel. Yet readers of the Gospel can draw some conclusions about this author which do affect the meaning of Jesus as presented in this Gospel. These conclusions can offer some guidance to believers today as they seek to understand the person somehow behind this unusual interpretation of Jesus that is called the Gospel of John. Although he may always remain anonymous, he is not without character, personality, and contours. Something similar may be said of the community from which he came—or which he possibly founded.

The Passages

By now most people who have read the Fourth Gospel are at least aware of the Beloved Disciple. Whether he can be identified with the unnamed disciple in chapter 1:37 and in chapter 18:15 shall remain uncertain. Most will identify him with the unnamed disciple in chapter 18, but not with the unnamed disciple in the first chapter. This follows from the hypothesis that the Beloved Disciple lived in and around Jerusalem and knew Jesus from the ministry in Jerusalem.

13:23–26: He is at the Last Supper close to Jesus.

One of his disciples, whom Jesus loved, was lying close to the breast of Jesus; so Simon Peter beckoned to him and said, "Tell us who it is of whom he speaks." So lying thus, close to the breast of Jesus, he said to him, "Lord, who is it?"

19:26–27: He stands at the foot of the cross with the mother of Jesus.

When Jesus saw his mother, and the disciple whom he loved standing near, he said to his mother, "Woman, behold your son!" Then he said to the disciple, "Behold your mother!"

20:2–8: He outruns Peter to the tomb and believes.

[Mary Magdalene] went to Simon Peter and the other disciple, the one whom Jesus loved, and said to them,

"They have taken the Lord out of the tomb, and we do not know where they have laid him....They both ran, but the other disciple outran Peter and reached the tomb first;...Then the other disciple, who reached the tomb first, also went in, and he saw and believed.

21:7: He recognizes Jesus.

That disciple whom Jesus loved said to Peter, "It is the Lord!"

21:20: Peter questions Jesus concerning him.

Peter turned and saw following them the disciple whom Jesus loved, who had lain close to his breast at the supper and had said, "Lord, who is it that is going to betray you?"

21:23–24: The Beloved Disciple has died.

The saying spread abroad...that this disciple was not to die; yet Jesus did not say to him that he was not to die, but, "If it is my will that he remain until I come, what is that to you?"

From the passages a reader can conclude that whoever this disciple was, he had a close relationship to Jesus. He appears to be an eyewitness at least, from Jerusalem, who remained faithful to the end, and seems superior to Peter, at least as far as faith. He never denied Jesus and believed after just seeing the empty tomb. The community from which he came was quite fond of him and wanted his testimony to remain.

The Title *Beloved Disciple*

The response to the possible origin of these passages depends on one's opinion with regard to authorship. If the Beloved Disciple is the author of the Gospel, it seems unlikely he would have spoken of himself as the Beloved Disciple. Most will admit the Gospel went through various editions with different writers or editors. So, are these passages from the first edition, written by the Beloved Disciple, or a first edition written by another hand? Or were they added when the disciple had died, or some time in between? Were they coming from the life of Jesus, or from the community? Are they part literary to symbolize a historical person, or completely literary added to suit the needs of the final editor and/or the needs of the community?

Most likely the passages come from an author or editor who was not the Beloved Disciple. They are additions to what might have been an early edition of the Gospel written primarily for the needs of the community. Although this follower of Jesus probably did not call himself the Beloved Disciple, his own followers might have called him that, even in his lifetime. As in other instances in the New Testament, readers come face to face with the question of history.

Historicity

Hope for complete objectivity eludes all people living in any period of history. Objective history eluded those trying to retell the story of Abraham or Moses and the Exodus in the tenth century before Christ. The same remains true for those who attempted to pass on the Jesus tradition at the end of the first century of this era. How much of Jesus in the Fourth Gospel actually goes back to the historical Jesus? John Meier in his *A Marginal Jew,* vol. II, for example, makes a good case for the miracle of Cana to be a creation of the evangelist (934–49). Yet, mostly it is a beloved story in the Christian tradition and no one would think of throwing it out, precisely because it is liked—and the author did include the story in his Gospel, even if the author has composed it. The reality comes from the meaning and effect and not just the historicity.

In the Fourth Gospel more should probably be understood as history than many might want, but with less complete objectivity,

precisely because history is like a river. And less should be understood as history than others might want for the same reason. The
story means more than the facts. If the Beloved Disciple is so close
to Jesus in this Gospel, and if he is presented as superior to Peter,
even if this has little historical reality for the time of Jesus, it must
have had great historical value for the community of the Gospel.
But if the Gospel shows such interest in details, and if the community demanded acceptance, then somehow the testimony comes
from an eyewitness. Some history and some literary creation make
the most sense, both about Jesus and his ministry as well as about
the Beloved Disciple. This follower of Jesus had a history even if
the knowledge of this history is limited.

The Personality of the Beloved Disciple

Since the Beloved Disciple shows little interest in Galilee he
probably was not a Galilean. Fishermen are usually practical
people. This Gospel seems more contemplative. He was probably
not a fisherman. The author has a good command of Greek and
knows Aramaic and fills his work with irony and subtlety, and
even a forensic element. The author was "smart." He also seems to
have little interest in the apocalyptic doom and gloom. His interest
is in the present, NOW, and not in the future. Jesus does not suffer
in this Gospel. The author probably does not like suffering. Yet, he
acknowledges that Jesus died by crucifixion so he has some
thoughts on suffering which are positive. He sees a great value in
integrating suffering into human life. The Samaritans appear in
this Gospel in a good light and are treated with respect. Jews are
not. He had definite opinions about both groups. The Beloved Disciple seems to be superior to Peter, and to the Twelve in general,
since the word *twelve* is mentioned only four times and never in a
very positive light (John 6:67, 70, 71; 20:24). He seems to know
the geography of Samaria and Judea. The Beloved Disciple was
known to the high priest in Jerusalem. He probably liked to give
homilies and pass them off as the words of Jesus. Of course, some-

one could also say that the author or inspirer was a Galilean fisherman who did not like being one so he went to a good school and learned Greek. Later he wormed his way into social circles in Jerusalem, never quite made it as an apostle, and so passed himself off as superior to the Twelve in later life. The Gospel became part of the New Testament, and thus the church eventually recognized this testimony as appropriate, and the role of the Beloved Disciple as significant to early Christianity. The Gospel contains history, but who can be sure of how much?

Author or Inspiration

In the preceding paragraph, the efforts to unmask switch between the Beloved Disciple and the author. What were the words of the Beloved Disciple, and what were the words of the author or authors, and what were the words of Jesus? Most of the ideas, words, and phrases probably come from the Beloved Disciple but as preached by him, and not as written by him. As a founder of a community, he probably preached the meaning of Jesus frequently and during this period, some of his teachings were preserved and written down to eventually become the Fourth Gospel. The Beloved Disciple lived as not just one disciple among many but rather he seems identified with the tradition of this Gospel, even if he probably did not write it. The author presents him as a believer. No doubt. He follows Jesus, even to the cross; he is referred to as beloved; and he bears testimony. Each has some relevance to the historicity of both the Jesus tradition and the community—and the Beloved Disciple himself.

Believer

As believer, he sees the empty tomb and believes (John 20:6–9), in contrast to Peter. He is also superior to Thomas who needs to see physically (John 20:25). As a follower (disciple), he remained with Jesus to the end, joined only by the Mother of Jesus and some additional women followers (John 19:25–27). Prior to the cross, he followed Jesus to the court of the high priest (John 18:15) and since his appearance in chapter 21, followed Jesus after the resurrection as well.

Beloved

He is also beloved. This implies an intimacy with Jesus. He reclines close to Jesus at the Last Supper. He listens to Jesus from the cross and completed his intimacy with Jesus with the responsibility of taking care of the Mother of Jesus (John 19:26–27). The author singles him out for special affection for Jesus and from Jesus. From the Last Supper to the cross, to the final chapter, the close relationship to Jesus remains constant.

Witness

Finally, he bears testimony or witness. The bond of love qualifies the Beloved Disciple to be a witness of Jesus to others so that they might believe and love. The Beloved Disciple witnessed to his community and preached the meaning of Jesus to them. The Gospel contains this ministry of witness (John 19:35). "This is the disciple who is bearing witness to these things and we know his testimony is true" (John 21:24). The Gospel preserves this testimony for all generations of Christians.

The Community of the Beloved Disciple

The community of the Beloved Disciple has been called a maverick community (Kysar). They taught faith in Jesus and the love of the brethren as the essential elements of Christianity. They have been accused of being antiauthority, antisacramental, and antichurch. In fact, the community was individualistic but not exclusively. It believed in sacraments but only as expressions of faith. It accepted authority, other than that of the Beloved Disciple, only if those in authority loved Jesus and were willing to die for the community. It emphasized the here and now, and human relationships. All of this is readily recognized in reading the Gospel (O'Grady: 129–39). This community clearly maintained a different approach to the Jesus tradition than other communities of the New Testament. It had its own grasp of the meaning of Jesus. It reached into the Jesus tradition and took what it wanted. The community handed on the words of Jesus, but in its own way.

The Word of God and the Words of Jesus

Each of the authors of the gospels makes free play with the words of Jesus. Even Mark, the earliest, is willing to add words to the teaching of Jesus to interpret the parable of the sower (Mark 4:10–20). Matthew feels no compunction in adding the direct command to Peter in chapter 16, and the solemn sending-out in 28. Luke also freely adds his own words to the words of Jesus. Even if the author of John takes greater freedom with the words of Jesus than the others, they all add their own words and the words of their communities to the words of Jesus. They all experienced the essential limitations of life, thought, and speech and added their own truth mediated by historical flux, community needs and norms, and cultural warrants. Jesus was the Word of God incarnate, and Jesus as Word remained with the community. When the early community spoke the Word of God to their own community, they spoke assured that they were speaking the one Word of God made man in the life of Jesus. Inspiration means that individuals could and did add to the words of Jesus as they saw necessary, precisely because of ever-mutable humanity. The community lived the alive Word of God.

The Community and the Beloved Disciple

Imagine a Christian community at the end of the first century. It comprised a mixed group hardly able to get along without some overreaching person of great charism. Some were half-Christians and half-Jews, low Christologists and high Christologists, Gnostics and half-Gnostics, superintelligent and barely educable. Some emphasized only divinity, others only humanity. Just think of a greatly mixed community, which also had problems with other Christian communities regarding such matters as authority, essentials, sacraments—and an individual who tried to keep them together. The phenomenon has existed in every era in every religious tradition. How could such a community survive?

The community of the Beloved Disciple survived only as long as the Beloved Disciple lived. They had their own ideas about Jesus and Christianity and they had the testimony of the Beloved Disciple in the Gospel.

1. They wanted to be accepted by other Christian communities just as they were. They claimed they had such a right because their leader was present with Jesus and could pick and choose from the Jesus tradition.

2. The Beloved Disciple wanted to preserve what was essential to the Jesus tradition, never forgetting the role of faith and love of the brethren.

3. He and his community wanted to make a contribution to early and then future Christianity. The witness had value and belonged.

4. The community and its leader refused to be marginalized even as they were marginalized. They did not mind being at the doorway of the then-developing church, but refused to be outside.

5. The leader was willing to compromise but not in what he believed were essentials.

6. The Beloved Disciple accepted the complexity of an individual human life, and even more so the complexity of communal life. Multiplicity and variety characterized

community life and no efforts to over-simplify helped. Jesus himself was too complex. Life—humanity—never remains static.

7. The Gospel recognized the role of a charismatic type of authority and leadership and acknowledged its limitations.

8. The Beloved Disciple and his community created a Gospel expressing all of the above, and he and the community disappeared from history because they lacked the means of continuity. History went on and swallowed them.

Conclusion: The Testimony Continues

This most unusual follower of Jesus, and his community, disappeared from history. Only the Gospel remains. Just paying attention to the words of the Gospel, however, offers much in knowing about both leader and community. How they lived and how they acted continue to preach the gospel of Jesus today. How they made this Gospel their own also preaches. The witness of the Beloved Disciple reminds all that the various Christian communities need to be accepted by other Christian communities just as they are. Essentials are more important than accidentals. Faith and love still constitute the true meaning of Jesus and his tradition. The incidentals and accidentals of centuries never should obscure faith and love. History makes evident what is more temporal than what has some semblance of continuity. Both individuals and individual Christian communities in different cultures make a contribution. The maverick community of John got its Gospel into the canon of the New Testament. Marginalizing any segment of the community impoverishes all. Yet, marginalizing itself can emphasize a forgotten truth: a blessing and a curse. Compromise helps but not always. Life is too complex and all still live in history. Too much gray perdures and too little black and white, in spite of all of the efforts to proclaim the latter as definitive. Charismatic leadership is good but not perfect. It does not last, and can be the most creative as well as the most destructive.

So who was the Beloved Disciple? No one knows. Some even think the Beloved Disciple was a woman. Whether male or female, the Beloved Disciple probably was a combination of historical figure and ideal follower. The story is more important than the fact. His community was probably a confused mixture without clear lines of authority other than the Beloved Disciple and the Spirit. The leadership was spontaneous and not just tolerating but accepting, appreciating, and celebrating all people. Both he and his community lived on the edge of early Christianity wanting to be part of the group, and yet wanting to preserve some sense of unique identity in this early period. Today he remains unknown, in the shadows of history. Somewhere in here, in the midst of confusion and division and differences, with faith and love as primary, the lesson lies. The Beloved Disciple continues to bear testimony, whoever he was.

Topics for Discussion

1. What are some of the characteristics of the Beloved Disciple that appeal to you?

2. What characteristics do you not like?

3. How do faith and love survive in Christianity?

4. The Beloved Disciple lived and died as a charismatic leader. What are your thoughts on this type of leadership?

5. Does this testimony cause troubles for the church?

6. Does it make any difference that the author is anonymous?

7. How does understanding the community help us understand the Beloved Disciple?

8. Would you like to have known the Beloved Disciple? If so, why?

Works Consulted

Brown, Raymond. *The Community of the Beloved Disciple.* New York: Paulist Press, 1979.

———. *The Gospel According to John.* New York: Doubleday, 1966, 1970.

Charlesworth, James H. *The Beloved Disciple.* Valley Forge, PA: Trinity Press International, 1995.

Culpepper, R. Alan. *John: The Son of Zebedee, the Life of a Legend.* Minneapolis: Fortress Press, 2000.

Grassi, Joseph. *The Secret Identity of the Beloved Disciple.* New York/Mahwah, NJ: Paulist Press, 1992.

Kysar, Robert. *John, the Maverick Gospel.* Atlanta: John Knox, 1976.

Meier, John. *A Marginal Jew,* vol. II. New York: Doubleday, 1994.

O'Grady, John F. *According to John: The Witness of the Beloved Disciple.* New York/Mahwah, NJ: Paulist Press, 1999.

Schmithals, W. "Die Lieblingsjunger-Redaktion." In *Johannesevangelium und Johannesbriefe.* Berlin: Walter de Gruyter, 1992, 222–59.

Schnackenburg, Rudolf. *The Gospel According to St. John.* New York: Herder, 1968, 1980, 1982.

Chapter Twelve

Paul

"I advanced in Judaism beyond many of my own age among my people, so extremely zealous was I for the traditions of my fathers"(Gal 1:14). [I was] "circumcised on the eighth day, of the people of Israel, of the tribe of Benjamin, a Hebrew born of the Hebrews; as to the law a Pharisee…" (Phil 3:5). But this same Paul in Greek circles, Saul in Jewish circles, experienced the risen Lord Jesus and changed history. The Hebrew, the Pharisee, the Roman, became a Christian and helped chart the course for the religion that circled the globe, formed western culture, transformed lives, and continues to exert its power for good, and sometimes for evil, in the lives of more than a billion people. Of the 657 pages of Greek text of the New Testament, almost one fourth comes from Paul. In addition almost one half of the content of the Acts of the Apostles deals with Paul. Yet this Hebrew, Pharisee, Roman citizen was not an original follower of Jesus, not an eyewitness, not someone who experienced Jesus in his ministry.

Understanding this complex individual has never been easy. His background, his mind, his experiences interact and ebb and flow together. No wonder that many Christians do not like Paul—or just leave Paul alone. Some think he is a chauvinist and claim that the second-class status of women in the church can be traced to him. How happy many American women were when they decided

174

to take their hats off in church and the male-dominated church went along. All this in spite of Paul's comments in 1 Corinthians: "…the head of a woman is her husband…but any woman who prays or prophesies with her head unveiled dishonors her head…a woman ought to have a veil…" (1 Cor 11:3–10). Paul certainly had definite opinions, even if some were not accepted by all.

Paul's background supported his various attitudes and ideas. He was a Jew that was educated as a Jew but living in a Greek environment, influenced by Jewish religion as well as by popular and refined culture. Paul was intelligent and committed, and given to flights of fancy expressed in enthralling poetry in some of his letters. Paul lived on the edge, never shrinking from a challenge. He made friends and enemies and claimed independence, but humbly accepted the outreach from those who loved him. Given to extremes, Paul would likely have made a first-class scoundrel, had he not decided to accept his experience of the risen Lord and become the apostle to the Gentiles.

Jewish Background

Paul began his life as a Jew and boasted of his pharisaic tradition. He was more Jewish than most and proud of it.

> …I advanced in Judaism beyond many of my own age among my people, so extremely zealous was I for the traditions of my fathers. (Gal 1:14)

> …[C]ircumcised on the eighth day, of the people of Israel, of the tribe of Benjamin, a Hebrew born of Hebrews, as to the law a Pharisee, as to zeal a persecutor of the church, as to righteousness under the law blameless. (Phil 3:5–6)

> Are they Hebrews? So am I. Are they Israelites? So am I. Are they descendants of Abraham? So am I. (2 Cor 11:22)

Throughout his writings he seems to think in Old Testament categories and frequently uses images from the Jewish scriptures. Paul believed that the one God spoke to humankind through the Jewish scriptural traditions, and continues to speak to humankind in the Jesus tradition. Almost all of the teaching of Paul about God and humankind finds its foundation in his Jewish background. Frequently he explicitly quotes from the Old Testament and seems to use the Greek translation (the Septuagint, LXX). Following the practice of other rabbis, Paul accommodates an Old Testament text, or gives a new interpretation, allegorizes it, or changes its context creating a unity between the Jewish traditions and the newer Jesus tradition.

In Acts (Acts 22:3), Luke states that Paul studied Judaism under Gamaliel, the son of Hillel, a rabbi at the time of Christ who was rather moderate with regard to the Law of Moses. A sympathetic or conciliatory attitude characterized Gamaliel as witnessed in the Acts:

> "…if this plan or this undertaking is of men, it will fail; but if it is of God, you will not be able to overthrow them. You might even be found opposing God!" (Acts 5:38–39)

Whether Paul studied under Gamaliel or not, whether he once planned to become a rabbi or not, he used a good deal of rabbinical exegesis in his letters. Citing Isaiah 49:8 in 2 Corinthians 6:2—For [God] says, "At the acceptable time I have listened to you, and helped you on the day of salvation." Behold, now is the acceptable time; behold, now is the day of salvation.—Paul refers to Jesus and to his followers. In Romans 5, Paul develops the image of Adam as a type of the one who is to come. Jesus becomes the second Adam. Paul demonstrates his rabbinic training in his use of the Old Testament as he preaches to Jews of the meaning of the gospel of Jesus.

Perhaps Paul grew tired of the moderation and conciliatory attitude associated with Gamaliel, for the Acts of the Apostles state that he was on the road to Damascus to persecute Christians and bring them back to Jerusalem in chains (Acts 9:1–2). To travel to Damascus, with the hope of bringing back captives, Paul must have had some authority. In all probability he had the support of the Sanhedrin in Jerusalem. They would have chosen delegates to represent them who were learned in the law and possessed some degree of eloquence. Paul had both. Paul the Jew traveled to Damascus and became Paul the Christian.

Paul the Cosmopolitan Greek from Tarsus

As noted, Paul used a Roman name in Greek circles and a Jewish name, Saul, in Jewish circles. He knew Greek and used the Old Testament in Greek. He wrote his letters in Greek and they show a good classical education. Often his mode of expression and composition show some influence from Greek rhetoric. The Greek style of argumentation called *diatribe* can also be found in his letters as Paul debates with an imaginary interlocutor. His life as Greek began in Tarsus.

Situated on the river Cydnus, Tarsus lies a few miles north of the Mediterranean just below a pass through the Tarsus Mountains in southeastern Asia Minor (Turkey). The location of the city as a crossroads in the ancient world made Tarsus a lively center of commerce and trade. Romans, Greeks, and traders from the East shared a common life at the stadium for games, at the baths, in the forum and marketplace. The theater also flourished with plays dealing with pride, guilt, vengeance, human passion, and grief. As a city of learning, Tarsus ranked with Alexandria and Athens. From this city came Athenodorus the Stoic who was tutor to Octavian Augustus. The city experienced as well the fading of the old gods of Mount Olympus and the introduction of the mystery religions of the East, with their magic and astrology and exotic cultic practices. All became part of the background of Paul, to be complemented by his Roman citizenship.

Paul the Roman

Paul was a Roman. In an empire of more than a hundred million people, only about five million were Roman citizens. For Paul to claim such heritage implies that his family came from a rather high station in life. He makes no reference to them and so probably they were not Christians. Their son, however, a Jew, had acquired Roman citizenship. The Roman Empire encompassed a universal hope for unity. From the Persian Gulf westward to the outposts of Britain, the empire prevailed. Paul envisioned a universal religion in a unified world. The *Pax Romana,* with its language, its system of communication, and its commerce, afforded the new religion ample opportunities for growth and development. The road system alone assisted the great apostle to the Gentiles to make his missionary journeys. Paul began his letter to the Romans acknowledging "I am under obligation both to Greeks and barbarians, both to the wise and foolish" (Rom 1:14). Born in a city forming a crossroads of the empire, the citizen of Rome developed a feeling for unity and universality. He saw Jesus of Nazareth as the one who could give peace and deliverance from sorrow as Caesar had given peace and deliverance from the sword. But above all, Paul was a believer.

Paul the Complex Believer

In every human life multiple facets express the complexity of the unifying person. The more that's known about someone's background—family, interests, education, experiences—the more chance there is to discover the unity of the person. Paul was probably more complex than most. The New Testament has some of his letters and others attributed to him. Luke, in the Acts, has his own image of Paul. His temperament was far from gentle. He boasted of his independence from the other apostles, confronted Peter, called people foolish, set rules and regulations, and the Jesus tradition was never again the same. The mixture of pharisaic Judaism and its devotion to the law, and apocalyptic Judaism with its call for fidelity in the midst of pain and suffering, intermingle in Paul the Christian. Greek culture and philosophy, and the cosmopolitan effects of a great Roman city also influenced Paul of Tarsus—Hebrew, Pharisee, and Roman. Just one of these influences could cause confusion, but when united in one person, any reader of Paul finds it difficult to truly understand the man. Judaism and Christianity alone brought conflict. Add culture and interests to this and trying to understand Paul's personality becomes ever more elusive.

Paul's Personality

Paul's personality fascinates. He lived life with power and zest. He gave himself to life and to God and finally to Jesus of Nazareth. Whatever he did, he did wholeheartedly. All of his energies became funneled into his way of living. The great persecutor became the great herald. He traversed the known world as an apostle to the nations. He wrote numerous letters, founded communities, offered guidance, established rules and guidelines, sent out other preachers, and formed systems of organization. God placed him on a certain path and Paul responded with all the energies of mind, body, and soul. Paul of Tarsus experienced the presence of the divine, the transcendent one, on the road to Damascus and he changed, as have the lives of hundreds of millions of people because of his teachings.

Paul on the Road to Damascus

Paul's personality called out for a religious experience. This happened on the road to Damascus and changed his life. The Acts of the Apostles contain three different accounts of the experience: Acts 9:1–19; 22:1–21; 26:1–32 (Stanley). Paul himself refers to this experience in Galatians 1:11–24 and 2 Corinthians 4:4–6. Luke's first account is a narrative that explains Paul's ministry as an apostle. In the second account Paul appears before the Jews in Jerusalem, and in the final account he appears before the Roman governor. The accounts by Paul himself in Galatians and Corinthians should be preferred in trying to understand the exact meaning this experience had for him. Luke offers his analysis of the experience, but the actual testimony is colored by his particular theology and Luke's need to offer testimony to future generations.

In the Acts, Paul travels to Damascus with letters empowering him to arrest Christians. On the way, a bright light blinds him. No single event, apart from the resurrection of Jesus, has determined the course of human history as much. The first account of the religious experience of Paul recorded by Luke seems to emphasize that Paul can be ranked with the other apostles because he has experienced the risen Lord. In the second account by Luke the emphasis on the light and the mention of glory reminds the reader of the death of Stephen, so perhaps in this account Luke wishes to emphasize the role of Paul as martyr or witness. Finally, in the third account, in Acts, Paul becomes the prophet calling for conversion and reform, a message common to all the prophets (Stanley: 315–38). In each instance, Luke depends upon his own theology and adapts the circumstances to suit his established purpose. This analysis does not imply that Luke knew of no historical circumstances describing the religious experience of Paul, but rather that he put these circumstances within his own perspective.

In the presence of the divine, the appropriate gesture is reverence demonstrated by falling to the ground. For Luke, Paul experienced the glory of God in Christ Jesus described as a light brighter than the sun at midday. Paul falls to the ground. Luke has Paul question, "Who are you?" with the answer, "I am Jesus...." Paul becomes the evangelist and, like Isaiah after his experience in the Temple, Paul is willing to do whatever the Lord requests: "What will you have me do?" In some translations of Philippians 3:12, Paul will write that Jesus "apprehended" him or "lay hold of" him.

Paul's contemporaries thought that his conversion was inexplicable: "And all who heard him were amazed and said, 'Is not this the man who made havoc in Jerusalem of those who called upon his name?'" (Acts 9:21). Something marvelous happened on the road to Damascus that changed Paul from a persecutor to an apostle.

Paul's Version

In Galatians 1:11–24, however, Paul offers few details of his conversion experience. He merely notes that he had been a persecutor and that God had chosen him from his birth (cf. Jer 1:5) and revealed his son to him. In 1 Corinthians 15:9, he acknowledged he had persecuted the church and experienced the grace of God. In 2 Corinthians 4:4–6, he alludes to the glory of God. From the references to his conversion in the actual letters of Paul, it seems that he considered himself the least of the apostles, that he was blessed by God with a revelation of Christ, and that he changed from a persecutor to an apostle, preaching with success all over the ancient world.

Winner or Loser?

But was Paul the great conqueror moving from victory to victory, or was he, rather, a voice crying in the wilderness that failed more frequently than triumphed? Just who is the real Paul, and what does he offer to the Christian faith today? Christians customarily think of Paul, the great apostle to the Gentiles, as moving from triumph to triumph. He had his religious experience and then began his missionary activities by preaching the gospel of salvation for all through faith. In fact, Paul may not have been as successful as thought. History makers often live and die as failures. Only later do many significant figures take on the role that was often denied them while alive. If Paul followed Jesus, then for even greater reasons no one should expect him to be a great success. Just as Jesus might be considered a failure in his ministry, the same might well be said for Paul. As Jesus triumphed in his resurrection, Paul would triumph only in death. This seems evident in the problems at Antioch.

Paul and Antioch

The dispute between Paul and Peter, and the debate on expectations of Gentile Christians that took place at Antioch, meant that the interpretation of faith coming from James and Jerusalem, which was other than that of Paul, would become normative. Paul and his understanding of the gospel would remain in his writings, but would not become the dominant understanding of the Jesus tradition. No one will ever understand Paul without understanding what happened in his dealings with Peter, James, and the Jewish/Christian community in Jerusalem and in Antioch.

Jerusalem and Antioch

In the beginning, Christianity struggled with the split between those who saw the teachings of Jesus as a continuation of the Jewish tradition, possessing a system of doctrine and a code of ethics, and those who saw the teachings of Jesus as a proclamation of the redemptive act of God in Jesus, by which God opened the way, through faith, to reconciliation. Surely any believer today will say that it can and should be both. One position, however, can predominate and for Paul, salvation through faith was the basis of this new "good news." Peter, James, and the Jerusalem community advocated a continuation of the Jewish system, and this approach ultimately became the prevailing position in the earliest centuries. Paul, and possibly the Johannine community, held on to the emphasis of salvation as God's great gift through faith. In reality, only a combination of both approaches can do justice to the teachings of Jesus.

The Historical Scenario

Most people consider the event described in Acts 15:1–29, the council of Jerusalem and its decree, as the same event referred to by Paul in Galatians 2:1–10. Such need not be the case (O'Grady: 26–36). First, any scenario describing Paul and his history should be taken from the letters of Paul and not from the Acts of the Apostles. Luke, as already noted, has his own perspective dictating his use of historical events. In the past, most people presumed that in writing Acts, Luke presented an accurate history of the events narrated. What was learned about Paul and his activities from the letters of Paul was set within the framework established by Luke. But Luke may not have had full or accurate historical detail, and even when he had such information, he made adjustments to fit his purpose.

Paul himself writes that after his conversion, he went to Jerusalem and conferred with Peter, remained with him for two weeks, and also met with James (Gal 1:18). Paul visited Jerusalem a second time (Gal 2:1–10) fourteen years later and conferred with the "three pillar apostles." By this time, Paul would have established churches among the Gentiles, and his meeting in Jerusalem concerned specifically his mission to the Gentiles and the gospel that he preached to them. The outcome of this conference, with the leading role played by Peter, was an assurance that what Paul preached to the Gentiles, in truth, exemplified a proper understanding of the one gospel of Jesus. And Paul, in turn, was "to remember the poor." Paul willingly accepted this request, and in this meeting no expectations of circumcision, no ritual or dietary or ethical demands, were to be made upon the Gentiles in accepting Christianity. Paul was satisfied with the outcome of the meeting and evidently left to continue his missionary activity.

Sometime later, Peter left Jerusalem and perhaps at that time James assumed the head of the Jewish/Christian community there. For some unknown reason, the matter of observance of the law again became an issue, and, with Peter and Paul absent, the

Jerusalem community formulated what has come to be called the Apostolic Decree as found in Acts 15. Gentiles were not obliged to observe circumcision but were to abstain from things sacrificed to idols, from blood, from what is strangled, and from unchastity (Acts 15:29 and 21:25). If Gentiles did not observe these regulations, then no table fellowship could be possible between Jewish Christians and Gentile Christians. Peter heard of the decision and evidently withdrew from table fellowship. Paul confronted Peter as recorded in Galatians 2:11–13 and accused him and Barnabas of insincerity. This dispute at Antioch seems unresolved, since Barnabas and Paul separate and Paul, still holding on to his agreement to provide for the poor, plans a visit to Jerusalem, anticipating difficulties both from the Jews and from the Jewish Christians. In Romans he appeals to this community which had close ties with the Jerusalem Church, to pray that he might "be delivered from the unbelievers in Judea, and that my service for Jerusalem might be acceptable to the saints" (Rom 15:30–31). The Apostolic Decree, formulated without Paul, was not accepted by Paul, for it veered away from the gospel of grace, salvation through faith. Evidently Paul left Antioch without any resolution of the requirements of Jewish observance for Gentiles, which in turn affected his understanding of the true meaning of the gospel (Achtemeier).

Paul the Failure

An earlier, and different, view held that the Council of Jerusalem was convened, and with Paul and Peter present they determined that Gentile Christians were free from circumcision but were obliged to observe those laws required by Leviticus for non-Hebrews living in the midst of Hebrews. Harmony was restored and Paul was free to continue his missionary activity in good conscience, free from any harassment by those who wanted to require all Christians to become Jews. All of this is reported in Acts 15:1–2. Paul continued his successful activity as missionary and, but for his arrest in Jerusalem, he would have continued his preaching in the West. It may be that Acts errs chronologically, but at least it was correct in portraying the eventual successful resolution of the conflict between Paul and the leaders of the Jerusalem Church. Even when he lost, Paul saw the need for unity in this early period of church history and even modified his opinion, as recorded in Romans.

To return to a possible historical scenario, the Apostolic Decree of Acts 15 may be understood not as the result of the conflict in Antioch, as recorded in Galatians 2:11–14, but as the cause. Luke hints that the dispute between Paul and Barnabas that resulted in their separation (Acts 15:36–40) was subsequent to the Jerusalem conference. Thus, the dispute at Antioch was the result of this conference. No future conference took place that could restore the fractured unity in Antioch. Paul, as noted, will seek that unity and promote that unity in his letter to the Romans, but only after he has expressed his opinion in Galatians.

Antioch

Up to this time, Paul felt secure he was preaching a gospel with the support of the Jerusalem Church and with the support of the Antioch community. After the dispute, he lost his power base in Antioch and, as Acts confirms, had to travel farther West hoping to find acceptance for his missionary preaching. Later, he wrote to the Romans willing to modify his views, but still maintaining his fundamental understanding of the gospel. The tension between Jewish and Gentile Christianity, which had been present from the beginning of the Christian mission as reported in Acts, was not completely resolved. Thus, Paul never preached to the Gentiles without this harassment from those who disputed his understanding of the gospel of Jesus Christ. He may have ended his career as an isolated figure whose theological insights and emphases were destined for decline in subsequent centuries.

Obviously the defeat of Paul at Antioch did not mean that Paul was eliminated from the memory of the church. He is a hero in the Acts and his letters have come down as authentic testimony to his understanding of the Jesus tradition. He was surely remembered as an apostle, a missionary, and martyr for the faith. But it is the latter that is remembered more than his teachings. Luke, in the Acts of the Apostles, replaces the historical Paul with Luke's particular theological perspective of Paul—the one who will compromise his view for the sake of the unity of the church and the church authorities in Jerusalem. He is pictured in Acts as a theologian who could give wholehearted approval to the Apostolic Decree. He is also pictured as the one who would dutifully return to Jerusalem and submit to the authorities there (Acts 21:20–26).

Conclusion: Paul the Victor

Paul lost the battle but not the war. The complex believer, the "A" personality type, the cosmopolitan preacher, the wounded healer, the annoying apostle, lives on in his writings. He continues to challenge the church to take into account the particular dimension of justification through faith alone. Paul was like Jeremiah. He had his anguish, his sting in the flesh, from which he prayed to be delivered (2 Cor 12:7–9); he had confidence in the moral coherence of the world; proclaimed the supreme sovereignty of God; had an ability to criticize what he believed was wrong, and maintained a bold conviction in hope. Even in his life, Paul lived by grace rather than by works. He boasted of his weakness, defeat, and peril. Those who rejected his doctrine of grace also criticized his life as an apostle. The controversies recorded in his letters give ample evidence of these people in the early church. His theology was actually experienced in his own life. He served a crucified savior. Paul could not be a triumphant apostle of such a savior. The ultimate triumph would be of grace. Paul would await that alone. The many-faceted apostle continues to provoke controversy, and will do so in the future until the law-free gospel of God's grace in Jesus reaches fulfillment and "God will be all in all" (1 Cor 15:28).

Topics for Discussion

1. If the triumphant Paul becomes less triumphant, how does this affect your thinking on Paul?

2. Does Paul help us in living a Christian life as a follower of the crucified Jesus?

3. Paul seems to have changed his mind and was willing to accept some compromise. Is compromise a virtue?

4. Various approaches have always characterized Christianity. What might this mean for the contemporary church?

5. How is the code of ethics and the system of doctrine easier than the gospel of freedom? How is the gospel of freedom easier than the code of ethics and the system of doctrine? What is a member of the church to think and do?

6. Should the positions of Peter and Paul always cause tension in the church? Which position seems to dominate today?

7. If unity is the value above all, how would this affect the ecumenical movement?

8. Defeat is not always an evil. What might this mean today in the contemporary church?

9. What aspects of Paul's personality are appealing? Which are not? Do any bother you?

10. Paul had many influences in his life and thought. How could one compare his experience to the contemporary world and how would this influence religious traditions?

Works Consulted

Achtemeier, Paul. *The Quest for Unity in the New Testament Church*. Philadelphia: Fortress Press, 1987.

Brown, Raymond, and John Meier. *Antioch and Rome.* New York: Paulist Press, 1983.

Buckley, Thomas. *Apostle to the Nations.* Boston: St. Paul Press, 1980.

Fitzmyer, Joseph, SJ. *Paul and His Theology.* Englewood Cliffs, NJ: Prentice Hall, 1987.

O'Grady, John F. *Pillars of Paul's Gospel.* New York/Mahwah, NJ: Paulist Press, 1992.

Stanley, David. "Paul's Conversion in Acts." *The Catholic Biblical Quarterly* 15 (1953): 315–38.

Chapter Thirteen

Judas Iscariot

In the heyday of parish missions preachers often used the image of Judas Iscariot to encourage people, especially men, to go to confession. No one wanted to be a modern-day Judas, the traitor, the betrayer of Jesus. The opprobrium remains today. Calling someone a "Judas" says much. But was Judas worse than the other apostles, especially Peter who denied Jesus publicly three times, and joined the others in fleeing at the presence of possible harm? Was thirty pieces of silver what Judas actually received, or was this an addition to the gospel from the early church, taken from the Old Testament? Someone had to assist the authorities, so was Judas just used by the scenario that God had planned? And of course, the final question: Was Judas covered by the words of Jesus: "Father, forgive them for they know not what they do"? (Luke 23–34).

Judas in the New Testament

The four gospels mention Judas twenty times. The Acts of the Apostles refers to him twice. Needless to say, the New Testament does not portray Judas in any positive light. Most people know him as the betrayer and most also think he was a thief. It seems he was the treasurer of the group, and keeping track of money always has its temptation. All four gospels refer to him as one of the

Twelve (Mark 14:10; Matt 26:14, 47; Luke 6:16; John 6:71), but he plays a limited role in the ministry of Jesus, unlike Peter, James, and John. His moment of fame comes at the end of the ministry of Jesus: the time of betrayal and the death of Jesus.

The New Testament uses five different forms of the name: Judas, in each gospel and in the Acts (Mark 14:43; Matt 26:25; Luke 22:47; Acts 1:16; John 13:29); Judas Iscarioth (Semitic form) or Iscariot (Greek form); the one called Judas Iscariot, in two gospels (Matt 26:14; Luke 22:47); and Judas son of Simon Iscariot; only in John (John 6:71; 13:2, 26). Evidently the early church did not know just how he was called in the ministry of Jesus. Nor did they know the meaning of Iscariot.

Iscariot/Iscarioth

Probably the addition of "Iscariot" distinguished Judas from other apostles and disciples that were also called Judas (Luke 6:16; Acts 1:3; John 14:22). Many interpretations of Iscariot have been offered over the centuries. The word can be geographical, designating the town from which he came. It can also come from a word meaning "dagger-carrying assassins," and meaning that Judas was a Zealot party member. The word also may come from the Hebrew word meaning "false one"; or finally, perhaps the word came from both Greek and Hebrew, meaning the one who "handed over" [Jesus]. At this point individuals can pick and choose the meaning that makes more sense to them (Klassen: 1091–92; Limbeck: 200–201). Usually the simplest explanation responds best to the question. "Iscariot" probably designated Judas' place of origin, but not without some sense of a relationship to the Zealots, and the name somehow relates to what Judas did.

What Did Judas Do?

Judas betrayed Jesus to the authorities with a kiss. But was it really that? Paul mentions that Jesus was "handed over" (1 Cor

11:27) but leaves the betrayer unnamed. In Romans 8:32, God delivers over Jesus, and in Galatians 2:20, Jesus delivers himself over. In recent studies on the layers of tradition underlying the Synoptic Gospels, most concluded that Judas was truly a historical figure and one of the Twelve—and thus not created by the evangelists, nor a literary symbol of anyone who betrays Jesus. Although he may function in this capacity in the Fourth Gospel, Matthew, Luke, and Mark were not eyewitnesses, and so should not be taken as always historically accurate. The author of the Fourth Gospel probably was an eyewitness (Brown: 31; O'Grady: 64) and he clearly presents Judas as a betrayer (John 13; 18). Missing from the earliest traditions is the notion of Judas as the paid informer who ultimately commits suicide. The Gospel of John clearly presents Judas as the first one who left Jesus (John 13:30). The others, except for the Beloved Disciple, will abandon him later. With the later need for responsibility and lessening of the guilt of the other members of the Twelve, Judas becomes the arch villain.

Judas in Mark

The first gospel makes little of Judas. He was the one who handed Jesus over (Mark 3:19; 14:10, 44). The oldest part of the tradition in Mark connects Judas to the arrest in the garden in 14:43–46. The leaders seize Jesus. Judas is present but plays no particular role. The author does refer to the kiss as the sign (Mark 14:44), and Judas is not called Iscariot. Earlier, Mark has Judas present at the Last Supper, since Jesus predicts that one of those present will betray him (Mark 14:17). Then Mark states that such a betrayal will bring misfortune to the betrayer (Mark 14:21). Mark also mentions the financial reward. They "promised to give him money" (Mark 14:10). Mark follows the tradition that one of those closest to Jesus betrayed him. The traitor was not an outsider but an insider who even participated in the Last Supper. The death of Jesus was no accident but according to the divine plan, and Judas fit into this course of events.

Judas in Matthew

Matthew basically follows the Markan tradition, but adds his own interpretation. In 26:14–16 Matthew specifically comments that Judas received money for his betrayal. Alone among the gospels, Matthew gives the exact sum, thirty pieces of silver, the value placed on a slave in Exodus 21:32. In Zechariah 11:12, thirty pieces of silver is the wage of the shepherd who accepts the money and then on instruction from God, casts the coins back into the treasury (Zech 11:13). No one can be sure of the value of the money since Matthew does not mention the coin. Judas repents and confesses his sin (Matt 27:3–10) and tries to return the money he received. Then he goes out to hang himself (Matt 27:5). In this Gospel Jesus relates to Judas with gentleness and even calls Judas friend (Matt 26:50). When Matthew uses this appellation, however, it always refers to one who is ungrateful in the presence of generosity (Matt 20:13; 22:12). Judas seems more perverse in Matthew since Jesus treats Judas with great kindness. Even though he has already initiated his plan of betrayal (Matt 26:14–16), Judas still attends the meal. Matthew increases the portrayal of Judas as evil in Judas' final act of despair in killing himself.

Judas in Luke/Acts

Luke continues to add to the original tradition about Judas. He specifically comments that Satan entered into Judas (Luke 22:3). Judas also acts in consort with the Jewish leaders. They are afraid of the crowds and so seek another method to apprehend Jesus. Judas provides the opportunity (Luke 19:47; 20:19). In the background Satan seems to call the shots.

At the Last Supper, Judas stays to the end and is not unmasked as the traitor (Luke 22:21–23). Then the disciples embark on a discussion on who is the greatest (Luke 22:24–27). Perhaps Luke wants to place the betrayal of Judas in the context of the betrayal of the others as well. In the garden scene Judas leads the crowds, and although he does not explicitly kiss Jesus, he seems prepared to do just that (Luke 22:47–48). Jesus adds the comment about the hour of darkness (Luke 22:53). He who came to bring people out of darkness is under the power of darkness because of the treachery of the Jewish leaders, as well as one of the Twelve.

In the Acts of the Apostles, Luke adds little to the tradition about Judas. Peter remarks that the act of Judas was the way in which Scripture was fulfilled. Nothing is said about the actual betrayal. Peter speaks of Judas as acting as a guide for those who arrested Jesus (Acts 1:16). As for the death of Judas, neither Matthew nor Luke can be held as historically accurate (Acts 1:18–19). Luke actually joins the death to two Old Testament passages (Ps 69:26 and Ps 109:8).

Luke added Satan as the supernatural element, to explain the betrayal, arrest, and death of Jesus. Satan, in Judas, is then present at the Last Supper. Under the power of darkness, Judas ends his own life, even though he had functioned as one of the Twelve and had shared in the ministry of Jesus and the Twelve (Acts 1:17).

Judas in John

Five times Judas appears in the Fourth Gospel, and in many ways this Gospel has more to say about Judas than the other four. The first appearance occurs after the feeding of the crowds in chapter 6, and after Jesus has spoken of his body as food to eat and his blood as drink (John 6:60–71). Some found the saying hard and no longer followed Jesus. For the first time John mentions the Twelve and Jesus asks them if they wish to go away. Immediately after the reply of Peter that they have no place to go and are believers, the author places on the lips of Jesus the first prediction of betrayal by Judas. Here also Jesus says that one of them is a devil (John 6:70), speaking of Judas.

In chapter 12:1–8, John joins the other gospels in narrating the anointing, but while the other gospels mention that some of the disciples complain about the waste of money, John names Judas as the one. He also refers to him as "Iscariot," adding "the one who was to betray him." John also added the remark that Judas was a thief, and the treasurer of the group (John 12:6).

At the Last Supper Judas also appears. The author reminds the readers that the devil had already entered into Judas (John 13:2). He seems to participate in the foot washing without hesitation. Satan entered into Judas after receiving the bread (John 13:27) and after the dialogue between Jesus and the Beloved Disciple. Jesus tells Judas to do quickly what he has to do and Judas goes into the darkness (John 13:30). Although not present, Judas also finds remembrance in chapter 17 when Jesus says in his prayer that no one of them is lost except the son of perdition (John 17:12). All happened to fulfill the Scripture. Finally, Judas leads the contingent of soldiers with lanterns and clubs to arrest Jesus in the garden. Always under control in this Gospel, Jesus identifies himself, and when he uses the theandric expression "I am," all fittingly fall to the ground (Collins: 119).

The evangelist includes elements of the Judas tradition as found in the other gospels, but in reality Judas is not necessary. Jesus goes his own way. Judas, like Nicodemus in this Gospel, comes from the darkness (John 3:3) and fails to remain in the light. Judas aligned himself with the Jewish leaders who also prefer the darkness (John 9:39–41). Jesus remains the light coming into the world which the darkness cannot comprehend nor destroy (John 1:5). Judas represents the darkness of those who refuse to believe that Jesus is the human face of God (John 12:45; 14:9). They prefer darkness and into the darkness they go and remain. More than a betrayer, Judas represents those who will not believe.

Post-Apostolic Writings

Later writings from the post-apostolic period, and writings among the apocryphal works, continue to mention Judas in an unfavorable light (Klassen: 1095). A gospel of Judas also seems to have existed. Although no part of this work exists today, Irenaeus, Theodoret, and Epiphanius make mention of it. Probably written by a group of Gnostics, Judas seems to have had some kind of rehabilitation among them. Judas, by handing Jesus over, accomplished much good: human salvation. Evidently some in the early church treated Judas more kindly, instead of portraying him as being possessed by Satan or the Devil.

Conclusion

Judas as a historical person lies buried in the polemics of early Christianity trying to grow in the understanding of the death of Jesus. Like the other disciples, the failure of Jesus to use his powers to confront and destroy his enemies also destroyed many hopes, including those of Judas. Did Judas want Jesus to confound his enemies? Did Judas try to prod Jesus into action and never intended him to be arrested and crucified? Did Judas fail by his decision to pressure Jesus into restoring the kingdom of Israel and destroying evil? Did Judas fail by not realizing the type of Messiah Jesus chose to be? And when he realized that Jesus would actually die, did he then feel remorse for what he had put into play?

Judas surely represents those who refuse to believe, refuse to accept Jesus as the unveiling of God, as especially represented in the Fourth Gospel. But is this the real Judas? No wonder he continues to fascinate some writers and artists and even producers of Broadway plays such as *Jesus Christ Superstar* and *Godspell*. In a time of rehabilitation for many, even Judas seems to have his supporters. For all times, however, Judas will be remembered as the traitor, no matter how many may try to understand him. Tragic figures appear frequently in the Bible and in Christianity. Judas is one of them. This does not mean, however, that Judas was not included in the words of Jesus: "Father, forgive them; for they know not what they do" (Luke 23:34).

Topics for Discussion

1. Why should anyone pay attention to Judas?

2. Does Judas make you feel uncomfortable?

3. How many people have betrayed Jesus?

4. Does forgiveness apply to Judas?

5. Do you think Judas got in over his head?

6. Would the early church have wanted to portray Judas in as evil a way as possible?

7. What can Christians learn from Judas?

8. Why do you think this chapter has been placed last in the book?

Works Consulted

Brown, Raymond. *The Community of the Beloved Disciple.* New York: Paulist Press, 1979.

Collins, Raymond. "Representative Figures of the Fourth Gospel." *Downside Review* 94 (1976): 118–32.

Klassen, William. "Judas Iscariot," *The Anchor Bible Dictionary.* New York: Doubleday, 1992, 1091–96.

Limbeck, M. "Iskarioth, Iskariotaes," *Exegetical Dictionary of the New Testament.* Grand Rapids: Eerdmans, 1991, 200-201.

O'Grady, John. "The Role of the Beloved Disciple." *Biblical Theology Bulletin* 9 (1979): 58–65.

Epilogue

People make history. Different personalities and different historical periods interact to create lasting effects. Who knows how Jesus would have lived if he were born in the United States in 1960 rather than first-century Palestine? Who knows how Paul would have survived in contemporary New York? How would David have lived and died if he were born in seventeenth-century France? The popular acronym WWJD (What would Jesus do?) may appeal to young people, but does not easily respond to contemporary questions. This is not first-century Palestine. Each biblical personality comes from a particular time and place and who they are makes sense only within that particular time and place frame. The limitations of history, however, do not mean that these persons, these men in the Bible, have nothing to say to people today.

No one is perfect. Yet in the midst of human imperfection greatness can exist and flourish. Such is true for most of the individuals studied. Much has changed in three thousand years, but much also has remained the same. People still sin through the misuse of power, the poor treatment of others, the lack of justice and fairness, and the exploitation of the weak. Power, sex, and money still fascinate and can bring as much darkness as light into anyone's life. Unfortunately, for most, the darkness often obscures the light.

Apart from Jesus, and perhaps the Beloved Disciple, every man studied here showed serious flaws. Yet they are part of human history and religious history, and each has left his mark.

For most, the mark has more good qualities than bad. They lie buried in a book, the Bible, waiting for someone to read about them and learn.

> Men should not try to take on God. Better to go along. God is bigger.

> Men can talk to God as they will. Even being angry is acceptable.

> Men can sin greatly and trust in God more.

> Men should learn to accept the consequences of their actions and not hide from them or deny them.

> Men need never despair. God forgives more than humans forgive.

> Men need to pay attention to fidelity even in the midst of infidelity. God does.

> Men should enjoy life as much as possible. Life will bring its own down days.

> Men can learn to sit on a pile of rubble and believe that it will be rebuilt; the desert will blossom.

> Men can be "A" personality types and still enjoy life as they accomplish much.

> Men can learn to announce others rather than themselves.

All of the above statements, of course, apply to women as well. What is true for Adam, for the most part, is true for Eve. But men and women do respond differently in many aspects of human life. Differences remain. Both women and men, however, can see in Jesus of Nazareth something of themselves, for they are created in the image and likeness of God, and without this act of God as a foundation for both women and men, there never would have been a Jesus of Nazareth.

Epilogue

Reading and studying this book makes no sense unless the reader has also read Genesis, Exodus, 1 and 2 Samuel, 1 Chronicles, Isaiah, and Jeremiah from the Old Testament. From the New Testament the reader should have read the Gospels, the Acts of the Apostles, and at least Galatians, Romans, 1 Corinthians, and Philippians. The men come alive as you read their stories.